Art Direction: Thomas Boucher
Illustrations: Stephen Davis
Design: Thomas Boucher

Library of Congress Cataloging-in-Publication Data is available upon request.
ISBN: 9781947458802

Duopress books are available at special discounts when purchased in bulk
for sales promotions as well as for fund-raising or educational use. Special
editions can be created to specification.
Contact us at hello@duopressbooks.com for more information.

The author has independently reviewed the products referred to and compiled
in this book. No endorsement or sponsorship for this book by any of the
manufacturers has been given or is implied. All trademarks and trade names of
products and product manufacturers are the property of their respective owners
and licensors.

Manufactured in China
10 9 8 7 6 5 4 3 2 1

Duopress LLC. 8 Market Place, Suite 300 Baltimore, MD 21202
Distributed by Workman Publishing Company, Inc.
Published simultaneously in Canada by Thomas Allen & Son Limited.
To order: hello@duopressbooks.com
www.duopressbooks.com
www.workman.com

The

MODERN GENTLEMAN

*A Guide to the Best Drinks,
Food, and Accessories*

JOHN MCCARTHY

Illustrated by Stephen Davis

dp
duopress

This work is dedicated to my Dad, who taught me far more important things about being a gentleman than fine food, wines, and spirits.

—John McCarthy

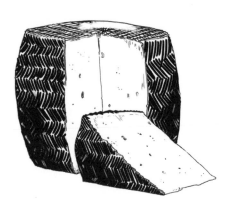

CONTENTS

PART ONE: DRINKS

PART TWO: FOOD

PART THREE: CIGARS

INTRODUCTION: THE GENTLEMAN'S GUIDE TO A FEW OF LIFE'S FINEST THINGS

Fifteen years ago, I didn't have a clue about a lot of the stuff you'll find inside this book. I couldn't tell you how cheese was made or how to order the tastiest oysters, and I didn't have any idea what the hell mezcal was. Not that it was all my fault. The '80s and '90s were not the best of times for craft and artisanal movements. Flavored vodka ruled the spirits world by significant margins (vodka is still the most popular spirit in America), and nobody I knew of was drinking fine rums or whiskey. Craft beer was in its infancy. My idea of quality tequila actually involved a worm. These were dark days. But then things changed in a big way. With the new millennium came an artisanal renaissance in how we raise, prepare, and think about our food and drinks. It was a movement I was privy to when I became the managing editor of *Men's Health* magazine in 2008. It was then that I noticed that while the brand was covering food and craft beer, nobody was talking about the whiskey revival or craft cocktail revolution that was in full swing. I saw the opportunity, claimed the category, and never looked back. For ten years now I have been immersed in studying the art of hospitality and the foods, spirits, and cocktails that make people happy. I travel the world visiting the sources of incredible agricultural products, and when I'm not on the road I tend bar and study mixology in a quest to master the art of making cocktails. I'm educating myself on the craft from both sides of the fence.

Much of what I've learned is condensed in the pages that follow. This book is designed to enhance your life by imparting a deeper understanding of the things we already enjoy. Each chapter represents an entry point into a curated category—beer, cocktails, and hot sauce are just a few. When you develop a knowledge of one of the world's great products, be it cheese, wine, whiskey, or a nice cigar, the reward is a deeper appreciation of these things. From there, it's only natural that you will start to enjoy them more. That is the pathway toward elevating your experiences to a higher plane and becoming a true modern gentleman.

For example, look at bourbon enthusiasts. You've tasted your way through the good stuff, maybe read Fred Minnick's blog, got the lowdown on how it's all made, and now you feel like you are part of the bourbon community. Now that you "get it," you're ready to graduate to the next level—so where do you go? The answer is simple: you go to the source. A distillery trip to Kentucky allows you to learn the distillation process firsthand by seeing for yourself how all that delicious whiskey gets made. Go to a rackhouse and take in the powerful aroma of thousands of oak barrels aging. Every time you sniff the whiskey in your glass, you can go back there. It transcends you. Now you're enjoying your bourbon on a whole other level.

The same ethereal experiences apply to every chapter in this book, from wine (how about a trip to Napa, Tuscany, or the Loire Valley in southern France?) to charcuterie (discover what makes Iberico ham from Spain taste so special). One thing people ask me is how to tell if a product is the real deal or just commercial fare in fancy wrapping. It's a legitimate concern. The reality is that misleading marketing and misinformation are rampant in every category, so one of the goals of this book is to help you spot authenticity from its imposters. Here's a hint: it usually involves reading the label.

Being a modern gentleman boils down to procuring and enjoying the best efforts of skilled chefs, farmers, fishermen, craftsmen, and distillers, who are using the best ingredients and often preserving traditions to produce food for enjoyment, not economy. The celebration of these crafts is what this book is all about, and your reward for educating yourself more deeply is the opportunity to enjoy the things that taste good and that sometimes get you buzzed. Speaking of getting buzzed, I talk about drinking quite a bit in this book, and I just want to remind you that while enjoying a damn fine whiskey is one of life's most exquisite pleasures, it's easy to get carried away. Alcohol helps create a fun-filled ride through life, but it also has the power to ruin it. Respect is key.

Foodies, bon vivants, aficionados, connoisseurs, gastronomists, gourmands, and influential types come from all walks of life—and there will be no judgments or hipster bullshit here. This book is devoid of advice about how to dress, cut your hair, or curl your mustache. Who you are and how you present yourself is entirely up to you. Excellent grooming, working out, optimal nutrition, and dressing well all contribute to your efforts to live your best life, but advice on those is probably best left for another book. This one's all about the creature comforts, and you will find that I like to drive home one point above all when exploring the finest offerings in any category: try everything. Understand what you are eating or drinking. Then go with what tastes good to you. I hope you enjoy the book, but more importantly, I hope you can find new passions in which to indulge and make the effort to treat yourself well. You deserve it.

PART ONE: DRINKS

THE BEER EXPERT'S STARTER KIT

"Here's to alcohol. The cause of and solution to all of life's problems."

— *Homer Simpson*

Grain, hops, barley, and water. I have always loved beer. Even back in my early days of drinking, I understood that a tasty, cold brew on a hot summer day is one of life's most profound yet straightforward pleasures. But I wasn't picky. I was on a quest to find the cheapest possible way to get hammered, and sadly I spent many years subjecting myself to crappy beer. Don't make the same mistake. Good beer is everywhere. Every state in America now has a local brewing scene, and the U.S. is the world's largest producer of craft beer in the world. Ninety-two percent of Americans live within ten miles of a brewery that pumps out local versions of virtually every style. There's no excuse not to explore, indulge, and take chances.

The industry-recognized method of measuring the flavor of beer is called an International Bitterness Unit (IBU). The higher the IBU, the more bitter the beer. Your everyday big box lagers, like Budweiser, run about a somewhat spineless seven, while Guinness Stout clocks in at 40. Hoppy IPAs have an entire 100+ IBU category, and the world's hoppiest beers, like Dogfish Head Hoo Lawd, clock in north of 1,000. I cannot drink these.

The modern American beer culture has its milestones, but craft brewing began forty years ago when home brewing and winemaking were legalized by President Jimmy Carter in 1978. A grassroots microbrew movement evolved, eventually growing into the massive brew scene we enjoy today. But the unifying factor of most of these beers is that they are likely based on a classic European style, and understanding those styles is your key to unlocking the beer universe.

When tasting beer, pay attention to the following: astringency, body, carbonation, and length of finish, which ranges between 15 seconds to over 60. Identify flavors like fruity, floral, herbal, citrus, and spicy. And be cautious of ABV (alcohol by volume). Many crafts are double your standard mass-market lager and have knocked me on my butt more than once.

ALES, PALES, PORTERS, WHEATERS, AND STOUTS

Ale is the most common beer in the world and was the first to be brewed in America. It's also the easiest to brew, and the broadest range of styles fall into this category. Pale, brown, India pale, strong, porter, and Scottish ales are all significant styles in which dozens of variations reside.

PALE ALE

Sweet, dark porters and stouts dominated the English beer scene during the 19th century, but on the periphery, the pale ale, a "new style" brewed with lighter barley and a higher hop count, was emerging. Over a century later in the United States, Sierra Nevada Pale Ale is credited with sparking the American craft beer movement, making it the perfect baseline APA to compare against other American pales.

How Does It Taste: Look for classic malt flavors with spice and citrus notes imparted from the American-style hops on the finish and a 5.6% ABV and an IBU of 37. American pales are medium bodied and slightly higher in alcohol than English pales, with IBUs of between 30 and 60. American-style hops imparts notes of pine and citrus, which are signature flavor components in the modern style.

Try These: 3 Floyds Brewing Zombie Dust (Munster, IN), Sierra Nevada Pale (Chico, CA), Fort Point Double Dry Hopped Pale Ale (Trillium, Boston, MA), Six Point Sweet Action (Brooklyn, NY).

INDIA PALE ALE

The hottest style in the craft world right now is India pale ale, the mighty IPA. More than 32 million cases of IPA were sold in 2018, yet it remains as divisive as it is popular, with two acutely opinionated camps of lovers and haters. That's all just part of the fun with this bitter, floral, hoppy brew. IPAs came to be when the English upped the hop count as a preservative in beer being exported to British soldiers in India, and the extra-bitter brew caught on.

How Does It Taste: There are three major categories of IPA—English, American, and Imperial—which as a rule escalate from English being the least bitter, followed by American IPAs running between 30–60 IBU, while Imperial IPAs are often the hoppiest and intense at 60–100+ IBU.

Try These: Heady Topper Double IPA (Burlington, VT), the Alchemist Brewing Company (Stowe, VT), Nelson IPA and Widows Up (Alpine Beer Co., Alpine, CA), Project Dank (La Cumbre Brewing, Albuquerque, NM), Ballast Point Sculpin IPA (San Diego, CA), Green Flash Brewing Co's Imperial IPA (San Diego, CA), Juice Bomb IPA (Sloop Brewing, Elizaville, NY).

STOUTS AND PORTERS

Stouts are based on malted barley, deeply roasted to produce the darkest of all beers. Irish-born Guinness is the most famous. For a cream stout, brewers add lactose to lend creaminess to the mix. Porters are made with a recipe of dark, amber, and light barley, and they fall somewhere between a stout and an ale.

How Does It Taste: Porters take on stout's signature flavors of coffee and chocolate but are generally lighter and less bitter, with an IBU range of 16–20.

Try These: Founder's Breakfast Stout (New Holland Brewery Holland, MI), Oatmeal Yeti American Imperial Stout (Great Divide Brewing Company, Denver, CO), Goose Island Bourbon Country Brand Stout (Chicago, IL).

WHEAT BEERS

German brewers figured out long ago that adding wheat to a beer mash imparts a crisp effervescent mouthfeel that's not unlike the bubbles in Champagne. German Weissbier, a cloudy, yeasty Hefeweizen, is a popular style in the States that uses a high ratio of wheat to barley and a specific ale yeast that gives the beer a tart, dry quaff with low bitterness and a reasonable alcohol level of 5–7 percent.

Belgian witbier, or Belgian white, is a wheater flavored with spices like coriander and orange peel and has a slightly higher bitterness than its German cousins.

Try These: Dancing Man German Hefeweizen (New Glarus Brewing Company, New Glarus, WI), Wittekerke (De Brabandere, Belgium).

A BRIEF TIMELINE OF BEER HISTORY

· **7000 BCE** Chinese villagers consume the first known naturally fermented alcoholic beverage made of rice and fruit.

· **2500–3000 BCE** The first known beer recipe is written on tablets in Ebla, Syria, while the first chemical evidence of beer is found in clay pots in today's Iran.

· **822 CE** The first recorded use of hops in beer by Abbot Adalhard of the Benedictine monastery of Corbie, in France.

· **1000 CE** Beer gains popularity in medieval times since it is healthier than water, and it probably didn't hurt that everybody was smashed much of the time.

· **1420** Cold fermented lagers are invented, allegedly by mistake.

· **1516** A beer purity law called the Reinheitsgebot is instituted in Bavaria; it initially permits beer to be made only with three ingredients: barley, hops, and water. Later, yeast is acknowledged and wheat becomes allowed.

· **1573** Heinrich Knaust writes the first extensive book on brewing in Germany, describing in detail about 150 beers.

· **1632** Dutch explorers Adrian Block and Hans Christiansen open the first brewery in the United States on Stone Street, in New York City. The street is paved in stone to keep the beer wagons from sinking.

· **1721** The first known porter hits the scene in London.

· **1750** Modern mass-market brewing is born.

· **1759** Guinness is founded when Arthur Guinness buys a small brewery in Dublin. The brewery originally produces a variety of beers, but in 1799 the company decides to focus exclusively on porter, a dark beer with a creamy head.

· **1784** The first steam engine in London is installed in the Red Lion porter brewery.

· **1814** Tragedy strikes in London when 300,000 gallons of porter spill, killing eight people "by drowning, injury, poisoning, or drunkenness."

· **1844** John Wagner brings lager yeast with him from Bavaria to build the first lager brewery in the United States, in Philadelphia.

· **1876** The red triangle of the Bass brewery becomes the first trademark in England.

· **1920** Prohibition begins in the United States and lasts until 1933.

· **1935** Beer cans debut. Pull tabs don't come around until almost thirty years later.

· **1976** The first modern microbrewery, the New Albion Brewing Company, opens in Sonoma, California.

· **1978** The United States records only 89 breweries, the lowest point since the number was first recorded in 1873 (excluding Prohibition). Most of these are owned by six companies.

· **1978** President Jimmy Carter makes home brewing and winemaking legal; this is credited with sparking the craft revolution, which doesn't really start to peak until the '90s.

· **1984** Boston Beer Company is founded in Boston, Massachusetts. It will become the most successful independent craft beer producer in the country.

· **1994** Sierra Nevada becomes the first craft beer to be sold to a large brewer, opening the floodgates for hundreds of small producers to be swallowed up by big boys, getting wealthy in the process.

· **1998** Twenty years after a record low of 89 American breweries, the number surpasses 1,500, and craft brewing is in full swing.

· **2008** Big brewing is far from dead as Anheuser-Busch, producer of Budweiser and the largest brewery in the United States, is acquired by InBev, a Belgian-Brazilian brewing conglomerate, for $52 billion.

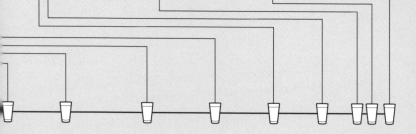

BELGIAN ABBEY AND TRAPPIST ALES

Despite its rep as a complex field, Belgian brew is easily demystified once you see that Belgian beer is the same as the ales and lagers the rest of Europe produces. Abbey ales are born of an ancient Belgian tradition where Trappist monks brewed beer for sustenance in a time when fresh water was unreliable. This tradition has been carried down for centuries. Today, "abbey ale" is an unprotected term with no guarantee of authenticity, but it doesn't mean the beer is bad. For a little more gravitas and authenticity, seek out Trappist beer labeled "Authentic Trappist Product." This guarantees that a beer was brewed at one of six active Belgian monasteries.

While light, quaffable "singel" ales were brewed for local consumption, the brewers amped up the color, flavor, and alcohol of their ale for an export called a dubbel (double), a dark ale with an alcohol content of 6–7.5%. A tripel is a golden ale that's even higher in strength and became the Belgian darling of American craft brewers. Tripels are traditionally made with sweet pilsner malt that is goosed with sugar to enhance fermentation. Some Belgian brewers, as well as their American counterparts, push the envelope further with quadrupel styles, amped-up versions of the tripel, which top out around 15% ABV.

How Does It Taste: The dubbel's deep brown hue comes from caramelized sugar, not roasted barley, lending a signature raisin-like sweetness to an otherwise dry brew whose low bitterness clocks in at 10–15 IBU. Tripels are all about malty fruit and bold carbonation.

Try These: Chimay Cinq Cents White Triple, Chimay Grande Reserve Blue, Chimay Premiere Red, Rochefort 10 Trappist Ale, Westmalle Dubbel, and Tripel Trappist Ale.

LAGERS, PILSNERS, AND BOCKS

LAGER

Look beyond the lightweight American big-box brewskis and seek out serious German lager, a family of iconic beers that range from light, golden pilsners to dark, heavy bocks. Lagers were developed in Germany with a cold fermentation process called lagering. A time-consuming method of fermenting coupled with cold storage aging produced a lighter, crisper *bier* than the warm, chewy English ales of the time.

The Reinheitsgebot of 1516 was the purity law brought forth by Duke Wilhelm IV of Bavaria (in today's Germany), which decreed that you may only brew beer with three ingredients: barley, hops, and water (yeast was later added to the list, and barley was changed to "grains"). This rule has remained for 500 years.

Try These: Hecate German-Style Dark Lager (Pueblo Vida Brewing Co., Tucson, AZ), Dancing Bear (Magic Rock Brewing, England), Cigar City Lager (Tampa, FL).

PILSNER

The most copied beer in modern history is Pilsner Urquell, the first Bohemian-style pilsner (or pilsener) from Plzen in the present-day Czech Republic, which serves as the base for hundreds of commercial brands. Created in 1847, the light, partially malted barley stands in contrast to the roasted barley German brewers favored. The Germans adopted the "pils," which predictably evolved into their style and became the most consumed beer in Germany. In the States, brewers borrow inspiration from both methods to create a range of pilsners running the gamut between light-bodied malt sweetness to rich, thick, caramel beers with a bitter backbite.

How Does It Taste: A well-made pilsner is a tough beer to perfect, and the best will display a solid head, balanced flavors, and a quick finish, with an ABV of around 5%. Look for light straw to golden orange color and expect a malty sweetness and a mid-range to higher bitterness of 25–45 IBU.

Try These: Legend Has It (Creature Comforts Brewing Co., Athens, GA), Industry Pils (Austin Beer Garden Brewing Co., Austin, TX), Kicking & Screaming Pilsner (Threes Brewing, Brooklyn, NY).

BOCKS

The roots of German bocks trace back to the 14th century in the city of Einbeck in northern Germany, which made this dark and potent lager. Today's updated classics haven't swayed too far. A bock's M.O. is a high malt sweetness and low to medium hop count with a strong alcohol content of 5–7%, brewed lager style, using cold storage fermentation. German-style maibock is strong amber beer brewed in the winter and drunk in the spring. Doppelbock, meaning "double-bock," was created at the Paulaner brewery in Munich and is a more aggressive strain of the classic that is slightly higher in alcohol and hop count than traditional bocks.

How Does It Taste: Bocks generally swing towards the sweet-malt side of the beer spectrum, the opposite of an IPA. Bocks range in color from amber to dark brown, with, as a rule, maibocks being paler and doppelbocks the darkest with an IBU range of under 20 and up to about 30.

Try These: Millstream Schokolade Bock (Millstream Brewing, IA), St. Nikolaus Bock Bier (Pennsylvania Brewing, PA), Salvator Doppelbock (Paulaner, Munich, Germany).

HOW TO SIGN A CREDIT CARD RECEIPT WITH STYLE

Here's a scenario that occurs millions of times a day throughout the world: You're with your friends or colleagues in a restaurant, and it's time to pay the bill. Chances are you're using a credit card, which your server has now processed and delivered back to you with a receipt to sign. In the black pleather book there sits a pen. Here's the thing: there's an excellent chance that this pen is disgusting. Nobody washes a pen, but it's being touched repeatedly all day by people who just had their hands in every manner of food. Since contracting salmonella or *E. coli* is no way to conclude a meal, your move here is simple: whip out your own piece. Not only is it more sanitary, but it's a perfect opportunity to flash a little class. Here are a few cool styles:

Shinola + Fisher Bullet Space Pen with Shinola Detroit Logo

It wasn't until I saw an episode of *Seinfeld*, the best show ever, that I realized that a pen doesn't write upside down. I guess I never tried it. But the impressive-looking Shinola + Fisher Bullet Space Pen was designed for use on spaceflights and has the capability to write upside down, in microgravity, and even underwater. Fish use them all the time. **$35**

Montblanc Meisterstück Platinum-Coated Classique

Montblanc is the Rolex of pens. There is no doubt that when you pull out this timeless classic it adds a little extra weight to your signature. While those in the know might throw you a nod of approval and those who don't might feel a pang of envy at a glimpse of a Meisterstück, consider this: while a wristwatch of equal value won't raise many eyebrows, this timeless ballpoint classic will. **$440**

Ballpark Seat Pens: Color Top

While the Shinola will make you feel like James Bond and the Montblanc makes an unspoken statement, these ballpark seat pens from Uncommon Goods are a conversation piece. I found these cool black-ink rollerballs made from the salvaged seats of historic baseball stadiums. The outside is a slick little nod to baseball history, especially if they've got your team. Not me, I'm a Mets fan. But Busch Stadium (St. Louis Cardinals), Comiskey Park (Chicago White Sox), Crosley Field (Cincinnati Reds), Dodger Stadium (Los Angeles Dodgers), Ebbets Field (Brooklyn Dodgers), Fenway Park (Boston Red Sox), Forbes Field (Pittsburgh Pirates), the Polo Grounds (New York Giants), RFK Stadium (Washington Senators), Seals Stadium (San Francisco Seals/Giants), Shibe Park (Philadelphia Athletics), Tiger Stadium (Detroit Tigers), Wrigley Field (Chicago Cubs), and Yankee Stadium (New York Yankees) are all on the menu. **$150–$190.**

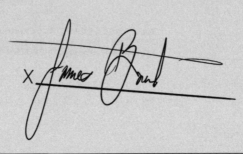

THE WORLD OF WINE

Wine had always intimidated me. I drank copious amounts of it back in the day, don't get me wrong. In fact, I still have trouble leaving an open bottle be. The thing was, as much as I loved wine, I had no idea how to choose one. I couldn't find a good value or pair it with a basic meal, let alone ponder the distinctions between Merlot and Cabernet. Red or white was my general level of sophistication, and I wasn't fond of white. But after learning a few fundamental truths about wine, the veil was lifted from this mysterious and sometimes confounding beverage, and things finally began to click. After pairing with the appropriate food, white wine started tasting good. Now I can't imagine life without a little Sauv Blanc in it. Truth is, enjoying wine can be as academic as you want it to be, but what's most important is that you try it all and stick with it.

I think of wine the way I feel about golf. Golf has one of the simplest concepts in all sports: hit a ball with a stick into a hole. But within those rudimentary confines exists a universe of variables that affect the ball's ability to reach that hole. This to me also sums up wine. The world's most mystifying beverage is, at its core, not complicated at all: the juice of crushed grapes is fermented with yeast and often aged in a cask or steel tank before bottling. That's it. But much like getting the ball into the cup, within wine's simple concept exist millions of variables that affect what ultimately ends up in your glass.

Like a weekend golfer, anybody can enjoy the game, regardless of your level of expertise. All that's required is a little knowledge of the grape and an adventurous spirit. Wine can be fussy, sure, but you don't need to be a sommelier to choose a great bottle. Learning a few rules while indulging in copious amounts of vino will build your skills to choose an excellent wine. After all, it's just a bunch of fermented grapes.

GET TO KNOW YOUR REGIONS FROM YOUR VARIETALS

When learning about wine, it's important to clear up the confounding way in which wines are identified. French and other European wines are predominantly named for the region in which they are produced. France's Burgundy, Bordeaux, and Champagne are all examples. In the United States, most wine is labeled by its predominant grape, called a varietal; Cabernet Sauvignon, Merlot, and Chardonnay are a few common varietals.

TASTING WINE AND FOOD

I am by no means a wine snob. Drink whatever you like, I say. Who am I to judge? My idea of a fine Cabernet came out of a box until I was 32. But when it comes to bringing wine and food together, I have seen the promised land. Wine is intended to be drunk with food, no doubt, and learning how to pair the two is a life skill many wish they possess but few do, and the payoff is a lifetime of heightened, sometimes ethereal meals.

The key to a well-balanced wine is harmony between its four flavor characteristics: sweet (sweetness), acid (sourness), tannin (bitterness), and alcohol (heat). These elements converge to create a dance of flavors that complement and contrast, brighten or subdue, and sometimes contradict a dish. But when food's bitterness, fat, salt, and spices come together with wine's body and flavors, the combination creates layers and complexity that make both the wine and the dish taste better.

WINES EVERY WINO KNOWS

RED WINE

CABERNET SAUVIGNON

The power and opulence of Cab Sauv make this grape the king of the wine jungle and are responsible for many of the world's most coveted vintages. The best of these big, full-bodied, and complex reds age for ten plus years, allowing the tannins, astringent compounds that establish structure and impart bitterness, to relax over time as the wine evolves into a beautiful, velvety liquid. Cabernet is present in French Bordeaux blends and is also prominent in wines from Northern California's Napa Valley and South Australia.

MERLOT

"No, if anyone orders merlot, I'm leaving." These seven words spouted by wine snob Miles, played by actor Paul Giamatti, in 1998's *Sideways* caused a correction in the wine market that sent Merlot sales plummeting. Not that California didn't deserve a kick in the ass for churning out a lot of subpar red, but it wasn't the grape's fault. This is a testament to the power of opinion when it comes to wine. Don't fall for it. If you like Merlot … drink it. I do, and so do serious connoisseurs.

Merlot is in the same vine family as Cabernet, but it's naturally drier, higher in acidity, and leaner than its beefy cousin. The grape thrives in most wine regions throughout the world, notably southwest France, Italy, Northern California, Chilé, and Long Island.

PINOT NOIR

Pinot Noir is rightfully enjoying the spotlight these days as a red-hot red wine, and chances are it's going to stay hot. Pinot is believed to be one of the oldest known vines and absolutely the most highly prized wine as it is the driving force behind world-class Burgundy reds. While French Pinot is the world standard, it's unlikely you will be getting your hands on a bottle of Romanée-Conti anytime soon, but there are amazing Pinots from the States to check out. Oregon Pinot from the Willamette Valley has emerged as a rich Pinot region creating some impressive wine, and Californian Pinots from colder climates like Russian River Valley, Carneros, and Sonoma are all spectacular.

Lighter in body and color and less structured than Cab Sauv or Merlot, Pinot is known for its subtle fruits like berries and cherries, but Pinots can also get funky, imparting earthy flavors like mushrooms, wet leaves, and tobacco.

BUY THIS!

Feel like a sommelier with a quality wine key and then develop skills to use it. I have gone through dozens, and my favorite is the sturdy, reliable Rabbit. $20.

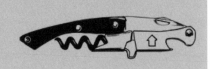

MALBEC

Malbec has long been one of the five blending grapes of France's infamous Bordeaux (the list is Cabernet Sauvignon, Cabernet Franc, Merlot, Petit Verdot, and Malbec), but its increasing inability to withstand the region's shifting weather conditions has caused Malbec to fade. Today very little if any ends up in the bottle. But in Mendoza, Argentina, Malbec is not part of a supporting cast—it's the star of the show. Since the 19th century Malbec has grown to become synonymous with fine Argentinian wine, with the best ones aging well over 20 years. From robust introductory wines to critically acclaimed stunners in the $50–100 range, Malbec is an excellent value for its quality and is a staple glass on wine lists of all levels.

Not too dry, not too fruity, Malbec is a full-bodied, medium tannin red with signature flavors of plums, blackberry, vanilla, and a bit of chocolate, often with a hint of smokiness that plays in the sandbox with smoky food, sausage, and cheeses. Beginning to see some crossover? That's because there is. There is no one answer when pairing wine. That's all part of what makes this fun.

> **Pro Tip:** When buying wine in a restaurant, expect a steep markup. To figure out a decent deal, bust out your cell phone and look up the retail price of the bottle. It should be no more than 3x the SRP in the liquor store. To figure it out by the glass, divide the cost by four. A $10 glass of wine should cost $40–$50 for the bottle, which should be worth about $15–$18 in the store. If it's an $8–$10 bottle, it's not a great deal.

WHITE WINE

CHARDONNAY

Low tannin, mid-range acidity, and a wide range of styles make Chard an approachable wine, approached so often in fact that it's the world's most popular white grape. Chards range in flavors from crispy, unoaked Chablis—a white Burgundy—to the oaky, buttery whites from California and other parts of the world where they employ a process called malolactic fermentation and oak aging to get it there. Things got so crazy in the '90s that the wine community has slowly been backing off the "malo" on Chard, but regardless of what the cork dorks say, people love it, so it's here to stay.

SAUVIGNON BLANC

If wines were cars, Chardonnay would be a comfy Cadillac and Sauv Blanc would be a slick Aston Martin. The French word *Sauvignon* translates to "wild," an apt description of this superstar wine's high acid and low tannic structure, producing a sharp, tart, head-turner that's so hot right now it's giving Chard a run for its money. The best Sauv Blanc comes from France's Loire Valley (where

Sancerre and Pouilly-Fumé are made), New Zealand, and Austria. Flavors range anywhere from grassy and herbal, to bright big melon and fruit, all the way to utter weirdness with occasional flavors and an aroma the French lovingly refer to as *pipi du chat*: cat pee.

Acid, fat, and salt play well together, and the crispy zing in Sauv Blanc has the power to counterpunch all sorts of rich and spicy dishes, think a Thai curry or Indian vindaloo.

RIESLING

I enjoy listening to people far smarter than me pontificate about the evils of "sweet" wines like Riesling, not realizing that many Rieslings aren't sweet. This conversation is best enjoyed while knocking back a clean, fruity Mosel with a kick-ass plate of spicy Indian food. While drinkers often dismiss this treasure, it's an absolute darling in the professional wine world since it has the bones to age for decades. Tons of acid is tamed by viscous citrus, fruit, and honey flavors that are occasionally corrupted in a good way with aromas of rubber and motor oil. All part of the fun. Dry Riesling from Germany is called Trocken, and the sweeter stuff will be labeled Kabinett, Spätlese, and Auslese. French Riesling from Alsace is typically dry.

Pairing Riesling: Riesling is perfect for spicy foods, and I don't just mean hot. Asian food laden with ginger, turmeric, soy sauce, and rice vinegar makes for a beautiful contrast to Riesling's intense fruit. It also goes nicely with roasted vegetables and all sorts of seafood. Especially Sushi. Yum.

Pro Tip: A sweet spot for purchasing wine is $15–$35. This way you are out of the basement where you will likely find wine made for efficiency, and you can stay away from the marketing departments' efforts to overprice bottles to round out a portfolio.

A BRIEF PRIMER ON ITALIAN WINE

The beautiful world of Italian wine is an expansive category worthy of a book of its own, but here is a quick primer on a few Italian bottles you will find at your local red sauce trattoria or upscale ristorante.

1. CHIANTI

Tucked into the hills of central Tuscany resides Chianti, one of the most beautiful regions I've ever visited and home of the infamous red Tuscan blend that's the most recognized Italian wine outside of Italy. You'll find herbal, fruit-forward, and leather flavors in a Chianti. Chianti wine is a must-have pairing with an Italian salumi plate or pizza. Secure a bonified Chianti Classico bottle by identifying Gallo Nero (black rooster) on the label. The better Chiantis are riservas, which are aged for at least two years.

2. BAROLO

Barolo is a potent and unpredictable red wine that's made from the Nebbiolo grape in Piedmont on Italy's northwestern border with France and Switzerland. Strawberry, roses, tar, and leather are your major flavors, and it has a deep, dark purple hue in the glass. Barolos are known for power, complexity, and sharp tannin structure so these wines can be cellared for decades and drink their best after a good bit of aging.

3. PROSECCO

America's favorite Italian sparkler is made primarily from the Glera grape in northern Italy's Spumante, Frizzante, and Tranquillo areas. Fun and fruity, Prosecco is made with classic carbonation as opposed to the champenoise style, making this wine less fussy and far less expensive than French Champagne; it is perfect for bubbly cocktails. Try a Bellini when white peaches are in season. Add about two tablespoons of the white peach pureé to a Champagne flute, top off with bubbles, and give it a gentle stir.

4. PINOT GRIGIO

Pinot Grigio is a grape varietal that is believed to be a mutant strain of Pinot Noir and is grown in the mountainous regions of Trentino–Alto Adige, Veneto, and Lombardy, Italy. Pinot is a light, flinty, dry wine with high acid and distinct minerality that's perfect with sushi, shellfish, and fatty, fried things. Considered a beginners wine, snobs turn up their noses at the pencil-necked pinot. But the fact is, if you serve it at a dinner party, it's always the first bottle to go.

BUBBLES! CHAMPAGNE

Yes, I know, Champagne is not a varietal. I was way older than I should have been when I even understood that Champagne—the undisputed king of all sparkling wine—was even wine at all. I never paid attention. Do yourself a favor and don't be me. Life is too short not to have Champagne in it.

Champagne is sparkling wine made in the Champagne region of France, about an hour and a half northeast of Paris. Champagne is made almost exclusively from Chardonnay, Pinot Noir, and Pinot Meunier grapes, and what makes this irresistibly fun and delicious sparkler unique is the ingenious method of double fermenting and carbonating the wine, known as the méthode champenoise style, where, long story short, yeast is placed inside the bottle, creating carbon dioxide, aka bubbles. When you pour out a glass look for distinct, toasty aromas on the nose, a signature of the style.

Pairing Champagne: Dry, light, and virtually nonexistent in tannin, Champagne is all about the acid, which gets the juices flowing before a meal, making it a perfect aperitif, especially with a plate of oysters or charcuterie and cheese to kick things off. Mac and cheese, ravioli, or any pasta really, plus any seafood from fish tacos to lobster are all on the menu. French fries are also perfect.

Pro Tip: To sleuth out what's known as a "grower" Champagne as opposed to a negotiant, who purchases grapes to make wine (note: this does not mean the wine isn't good), look for an "RM" on the label, which stands for Récoltant-Manipulant and means the producer and the grower are one in the same.

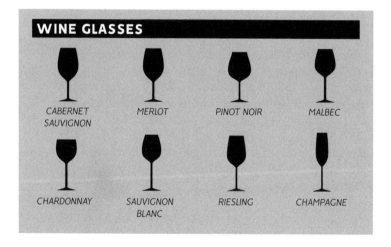

WINE GLASSES

CABERNET SAUVIGNON

MERLOT

PINOT NOIR

MALBEC

CHARDONNAY

SAUVIGNON BLANC

RIESLING

CHAMPAGNE

WINE LIST CHEAT SHEET

Red meat? Red wine. White meat like fish and chicken usually pairs well with white wine. Spicy food? Sweet wine. And while you can't go wrong with port and chocolate, you can go wrong with chocolate and Cabernet. Keep it simple: stick with port. Now you know a few rules, feel free to break them. As I said before, drink what you like. But to rock a wine list like a pro, it all begins with knowing a few tried-and-true flavor combos.

RED WINES

Pairing Merlot: Pork dishes, filet mignon, roasted chicken (See? We're breaking the rules already!), Chinese food, spaghetti with meatballs

Pairing Pinot Noir: Salmon, chicken, sausage, smoky ham, root vegetables, veal, duck

Pairing Malbec: Goat cheese, black beans, turkey leg, charcuterie, lean cuts of beef, chili, roasted pork, skirt steak with chimichurri sauce

WHITE WINES

Pairing Chardonnay: Lobster and shellfish, creamy chicken, pasta, vegetable dishes, turkey, veal, pork

Pairing Sauvignon Blanc: Thai curry, fried chicken, French fries, crab cakes, oysters, shrimp, scallops, snapper ceviche, green bean casserole, roasted asparagus, butternut squash soup

Pairing Riesling: Fresh white fish, roasted vegetables, sushi, goat cheese, spicy chicken wings, light appetizers, desserts

WHISK(E)Y, THE WATER OF LIFE

"They're all chickens!"

— *George Costanza*

I get all sorts of questions about whiskey. Sometimes I know the answer. Sometimes I don't. I do not declare to know everything about it, though I have, ahem, certainly tasted a few. While I often find myself the aficionado in the room, occasionally I'll find myself in one filled with experts who have forgotten more than I know. This is not only humbling, but an opportunity to learn, so I stay alert and ask questions. And to this crowd, my questions probably sound rudimentary. Maybe even stupid. Surely there are things I should know, but I'm learning all the time. I keep this in mind when people ask me "stupid" questions about whiskey. Suddenly they don't sound silly at all. Everybody's whiskey journey starts in the same place: the beginning.

WHAT'S THE DIFFERENCE BETWEEN SCOTCH, BOURBON, AND WHISKEY?

When I'm asked this question, inevitably a conversation from the '90s sitcom *Seinfeld* pops into my head. In the scene, George Costanza along with his father, Frank, and his future in-laws, the Rosses, were having dinner together for the first time:

Frank: *Let me understand. You got the hen, the chicken, and the rooster. The rooster goes with the chicken. So, who's having sex with the hen?*

George: *Why don't we talk about it another time?*

Frank: *But you see my point here? You only hear of a hen, a rooster, and a chicken. Something's missing!*

Mrs. Ross: *Something's missing all right.*

Mr. Ross: *They're all chickens. The rooster has sex with all of them.*

Frank: *That's perverse!*

Roosters, hens, or Rhode Island Reds ... they all fall under one banner: chickens. Just like scotch, bourbon, and rye are all part of one universe: whiskey. And what is whiskey? Essentially, it's distilled beer. Water, grain, and yeast, fermented and distilled—then usually aged in a barrel. The most common grains employed for whiskey are barley, rye, and corn. Different styles of whiskey are produced in different places, which is usually self-evident: Scotch comes from Scotland, Irish from Ireland, and Japanese from Japan. Bourbon and rye are products of the United States.

WHAT'S MY FAVORITE?

Easy. It's the one that's in my hand. Sounds like a punt, I know. But to me having a favorite whiskey is like having a favorite song. How can there just be one? When I am in the mood for sweet caramel and vanilla-laden bourbon that tastes as sweet as a Jerry Garcia ballad, then in that moment, that's my favorite. Sometimes I go for a smoky, decadent scotch, like I crave to hear "Ol '55" by Tom Waits every so often. When that happens, that's my favorite. No matter what mood I find myself in, chances are there is a whiskey to match it, and no one brand or style can sum up everything the world's finest spirit offers. Whether you're with friends, at a party, or enjoying a little armchair contemplation, there's a whiskey for that. And when the right whiskey matches the right occasion, it's the best whiskey in the world.

BOURBON, RYE, AND TENNESSEE WHISKEY

BOURBON AND TENNESSEE WHISKEY

Of all the finest whiskey, American whiskeys like rye and especially bourbon are dearest to my heart. Not that I don't appreciate the hell out of a beautiful single malt. I'm not an animal. But the aroma of vanilla, caramel, and spice-scented bourbon or a spicy, rambunctious rye laced with fruit and oak is what I most often end up drinking. It invokes memories. It reminds me of home.

Bourbon is a corn-based American-made whiskey that has been exploding as a category for years, generating over $3.6 billion in revenue for distillers in 2018. For whiskey to qualify as bourbon, there are strict regulations, so here are the basics to give you an idea of what's in the bottle:

Rule #1: Bourbon must be made from at least 51% corn. The rest of the recipe, called a mash bill, is usually comprised of rye for flavor and malted barley to aid fermentation.

Rule #2: Bourbon must be aged in charred, new oak barrels. This is important on many levels since a whiskey develops much of its flavor and all of its color from the interaction with the wood.

Rule #3: Whiskey labeled "straight bourbon" means it has matured for at least two years in said barrel. Any bourbon aged under four years must say so on the label. Most bourbon is aged at least four years. Hudson Baby Bourbon is an example.

Rule #4: While it's a myth that all bourbon must be made in Kentucky, it is required to be from the United States. It's the same principle for Tennessee whiskey, like George Dickel or Jack Daniels. Tennessee whiskey's trademark is charcoal mellowing, called the Lincoln County Process, a filtration process that "mellows" the distillate. But otherwise, it follows the same guidelines as bourbon and must be from the state of Tennessee to call itself such.

The reason these rules are important is because we the drinkers can rest assured that the color and viscosity (called mouthfeel) of bourbon is pure. Scotch whiskey offers no such assurances, and while many scotch whiskeys are not artificially colored, many of them are. This doesn't make them taste bad, it just makes their hue unreliable. Bourbon does not contain any additives like sugar, as you will find in rum and tequila. These are just a few examples to demonstrate that because producers are not legally permitted to adulterate bourbon, you can take it on its face.

There are well over a hundred flavors to be detected in bourbon. Banana, smoke, and cherry are a few I tend to pick up, along with the expected vanilla and caramel, plus familiar spices like nutmeg, cinnamon, and clove. Most of them are coming from one or a combination of three sources: the yeast strain, the barrel-aging process, and the mash bill.

There are three "standard" mash bill recipes employed in making bourbon that loosely define specific flavor characteristics of that whiskey: traditional, high rye, and wheat. A traditional method is a combination of corn, rye, and malted barley used by brands like Jim Beam, Heaven Hill, and Buffalo Trace and is in the neighborhood of 78% corn, 12% rye, and 10% barley. Mash bills with a greater rye content are called "high rye" and will take on more of the spicy rye character than a creamier, more traditional bourbon will, yielding a whiskey that's generally leaner, fruit forward, and spice driven. Bulleit, Basil Hayden, and Redemption High Rye Bourbon are examples. Wheated bourbons replace the traditional rye flavor grain with wheat, and you have a softer, rounder whiskey. Maker's Mark, Heaven Hill's Larceny, and the elusive Pappy Van Winkle are examples.

RYE

Before WWII, Maryland and Pennsylvania rye whiskey were as famous as bourbon from Kentucky. But the rye whiskey trade in those farming regions was staggered during Prohibition and knocked out by World War II when the government forced the distilleries to convert to ethanol plants to fuel the war effort. When the dust settled, distillers never recovered, and Maryland and Pennsylvania rye became almost extinct.

Seventy years later, the slump is gloriously over, and whiskey drinkers are rediscovering this spice- and fruit-driven spirit that is the base of so many classic cocktails like the Manhattan, and producers are happy to keep making more. Pennsylvania rye (Dad's Hat, Bristol) and Maryland rye (Sagamore Spirit, Baltimore) are making a comeback.

The federal protection of the rye label is identical to bourbon, except that the mash bill is in reverse. Straight rye must contain 51% rye and age for at least two years in a virgin oak barrel. On the palate, rye brings a whole other spectrum of flavors of fruit and spices to explore. Not spicy like cayenne pepper, it's more like baking spices; clove, cardamom, and of course, rye. Young rye tastes spicy because it runs a little hot, though black pepper is a flavor found in many ryes.

ICE, WATER, OR NEAT?

I am not a huge fan of telling you how to drink your whiskey. Neat, rocks, or in a highball, anyone who says you're drinking it wrong by adding ice or water should be ignored. As Fred Noe, Jim Beam's master distiller, puts it: "Drink it any damn way you like." The exception to this rule, of course, is super expensive whiskey, which everybody knows tastes best with Dr. Pepper. (Love that joke.)

SCOTCH WHISKEY

Scotch whiskey is the undisputed king of the whiskey world, and Scotland, from where all scotch hails, is home to over 125 distilleries housing over 20 million maturing casks that lie in wait to supply over 200 markets around the world, including much of the planet's rarest and finest stocks. Scotch is a lifelong passion for people who acquire a taste for balanced blends; funky, oily single malts; or the thousands of combinations of flavors and aromas within. So to decode one of the planet's most exceptional spirits, it takes a little bit of knowledge and much practice, which is, as usual, the fun part.

Scotch comes from five regions in Scotland: Highlands, Lowlands, Speyside, Campbeltown, and Islay. From those concentrated areas come two main styles: malt barley and grain whiskey. Combinations of the two result in five categories: single malt, blended, single grain, blended malt, and mixed grain.

SINGLE MALT

For a scotch to be labeled single malt, the whiskey must be bottled by one single distillery (single). It must be made with a mash bill of 100% malted barley (malt). Single malt must be distilled in a pot still and matured in oak for a minimum of three years on Scottish soil (scotch). Butts, port pipes, puncheons, Madeira drums, and predominantly ex-bourbon barrels are employed to age the whiskey, each of which tease out different spectrums of flavors, viscosity, and aromas. Age statements for single malts, as it is for all whiskey, must be the youngest juice in the bottle. It's common for single malt to be comprised of a blend of several vintages. A blend of single malts from different distilleries is called a blended malt. Compass Box is an example.

The most prolific single malt region is Speyside, which household name brands like the Macallan, Glenlivet, and Glenfiddich call home. In the surrounding Highlands, Glenmorangie (pronounced "orang-ey," like the fruit), the Dalmore, and Pulteney, a briny whiskey aged by the sea, are all excellent and diverse highland whiskeys. Campbelltown only has three distilleries in operation, the most notable being Springbank, which makes Springbank, Hazelburn, and Longrow. The lowlands are best known for blends and grain whiskey but are home to Auchentoshan, Bladnoch, and Glenkinchie single malts.

One thing all these whiskeys have in common is that they are all non-peated, meaning they don't have any smoke. Most of the smoky stuff comes from one of eight distilleries in Islay (pronounced "Eye-luh"), one of the most beautiful places I've ever seen. The distillery and the whiskey they make are Ardbeg, Bowmore, Bruichladdich, Bunnahabhain, Caol Ila, Kilchoma, Lagavulin, and Laphroaig. To make peated whiskey, the malt barley is smoked with peat, a dried deposit of vegetative matter found in damp regions like Islay, prior to distillation.

BLENDED SCOTCH

"I exclusively drink single malts," sniffs the preposterously pretentious man. "I like my whiskey smooth." And there it is. My cue that this guy has no idea what he is talking about. I mean sure, there are beautifully smooth single malts, try a chocolatey Glenmorangie Signet or a well-aged Dalmore; it melts like velvet on the tongue. But the whole point of blending whiskey is to showcase specific flavors while rounding out rough edges, making the whiskey complex, balanced, and often times, smoother than the sum of its parts. So screw you, Mr. Single Malt Snob. There is nothing wrong with blended scotch. When possible, reach for the good stuff. Something simple like Dewar's 15-year-old is delicious, or go nuts with a Royal Salute 21-year-old, Syndicate 58/6, or a little Johnny Walker Blue.

It wasn't terribly long ago that most of the single malt distilleries that sold whiskey to blenders were independent producers. Then large companies bought up most of them. But the idea of blending whiskey from different distilleries who specialize in different styles and distilleries trading whiskey among each other to create blends remains. A little sherry whiskey from Speyside blended with a base of lowland corn whiskey, spiked with a shot of peaty Islay to add layers of complexity is a simple recipe of a blend. Johnnie Walker Black Label is made of a combination of 40 different expressions. I enjoy it in a pinch.

IRISH WHISKEY

If you've never indulged in the joys of Irish whiskey, chances are you'll be trying it soon enough. There's a river of it heading our way. When the Tullamore D.E.W. facility opened in September of 2014, it became only the fifth major distillery in Ireland. One year later there were 14, and today there are close to 30 in some phase of production. This means there is a lot of liquid gold at the end of Ireland's rainbow, and once that juice is laid down and matured, it will be flooding the United States. Always on the hunt for something different and delicious, us whiskey lovers will have our cups out. Based on the beautiful products coming out of the Old Country now, it's gonna be one delicious ride.

Here's the deal with Irish. The vast majority (the signature style) are light, quaffable, triple-distilled blends of malted and unmalted barley and grains. Jameson, Powers, and Tullamore D.E.W. are examples. The result is easy sippins' compared to the more complex scotch offerings. But once you dig a little deeper, you'll find that Ireland has way more to offer than a shot of Jame-o. Here are a few of my favorite bottles in different styles to check out.

SINGLE POT STILL: REDBREAST

Single pot still whiskey refers to the inclusion of unmalted barley in the mash bill, not the amount of times it's been distilled, and while Jameson and Powers are examples, Midleton's Redbreast is an elegant, viscous, well-aged expression known for its spicy, grassy flavors.

SINGLE GRAIN: KILBEGGAN SINGLE GRAIN

A single grain Irish whiskey is one that's distilled and aged in a single location using a grain plus malted barley. In the case of Kilbeggan Single Grain, that grain is corn, which is double column-distilled to produce a leaner and softer whiskey than single pot still and takes on more wood influence than lighter, triple-distilled Irish. The result is a sweet, creamy whiskey bottled at 86 proof with enough familiar vanilla and caramel notes to lure bourbon fans to the Emerald Isle.

SINGLE MALT: BUSHMILLS

Bushmills White Label is the best known single malt Irish in the States. Check out their 10-, 16-, and 21-year-old age-stated whiskeys to appreciate an Irish single malt's potential. Malted barley is aged in ex-bourbon and sherry casks, marrying fruit-driven drops of heaven from the wine cask and caramel and vanilla magic from the American barrel.

JAPANESE WHISKEY

I recently had the good fortune of visiting Suntory's Yamazaki and Hakushu distilleries in Japan, where I toured the pristine grounds of these cutting-edge facilities to see for myself what makes Japanese whiskey tick. Japanese whiskey was born in the scotch style, and Suntory has three distilleries to create three distinctly different whiskey styles that may be inspired by Scotland but have flavors and nuances that are distinctly Japanese. Here are a few to sample.

①    ②    ③

① SINGLE MALT, UNPEATED: YAMAZAKI 12-YEAR-OLD

Yamazaki, Suntory's first whiskey distillery in Japan, is famous for its gorgeous, unpeated single malts, created in the distillery's 17 different pot stills. This is just one of the things that sets this whiskey apart from scotch single malt. Much like scotch, Yamzaki 12 is predominantly matured in new American oak and first-fill ex-bourbon barrels, then sweetened with Oloroso sherry casks from Spain, after which it is spiced up with mizunura, a Japanese oak barrel, and bottled at 86 proof, a touch higher than most scotch.

② SINGLE MALT, PEATED: HAKUSHU 12-YEAR-OLD

The Hakushu distillery is home to Suntory's Japanese peated single malts, the smoky stuff produced in the style of an Islay scotch. But unlike many of the potent scotch peat-monsters, the smoke on Hakushu is restrained, allowing the whiskey's herbal and green apple nose (how it smells) and its floral, tropical fruit flavors to shine.

③ BLENDED WHISKEY: SUNTORY HIBIKI HARMONY

Chita is Suntory's third distillery and focuses on lighter, grain-focused whiskey that serves as the base for Hibiki, Suntory's flagship blended whiskey in the States. Hakushu and Yamazaki stocks are layered on top of grain whiskey, like a chef seasons broth, before maturing it in American, Spanish, and Japanese oak mizunura casks. The result is a delicate balance of fruity, floral notes that will impress wizened whiskey geeks and delight Japanese newcomers.

WHISKEY OR WHISKY?

Notice that the word WHISKEY sometimes has an "e" and sometimes doesn't? Here's the deal: The Scottish, Canadians, and Japanese spell the word "whisky," while the Irish and most U.S. producers spell it "whiskey." Maker's Mark whisky is an exception. They just like to be different.

A FLASK FOR EVERY OCCASION

When I show up to a party strapped with a hip flask, friends have come to expect something special, a little tasting on the fly that adds a new, unexpected dimension to any gathering. I try not to disappoint, so I always bring enough to share. When I roll into a football stadium, I choose a slick flask for easy smuggling, just enough to warm the bones at a frigid and likely disappointing New York Jets game.

*Filson
Leather–Wrapped
Vermonter*

DENVER AND LIELY TRAVELLER

Australian glassware purveyors Denver and Liely built a killer 8 oz. stainless-steel traveller, whose tumbler-like design addresses airflow, temperature control, and palette delivery, so I don't have to. But what I love most is that it looks a bit curious, and, to me, uncommon is usually the most interesting. **$106**

FILSON LEATHER–WRAPPED VERMONTER

Whoever whips out this Vermonter ought to have some beautiful liquid inside. This tin-and-copper leather-wrapped 9 oz. flask is a serious statement piece that's designed by artist Jacob Bromwell for Filson, the high-end outdoors lifestyle company. **$345**

RABBIT DISCREET

Nothing fancy here, just a low-key 7.5 ounce tippler by quality barware purveyor Rabbit that's made of plastic, not metal, making it perfect for sneaking the good stuff into ball games and concerts. And if you do get busted, it's only gonna cost you **$10**.

TEQUILA AND MEZCAL

If you're not hip to pure agave spirits, clear your mind of everything you think you know about tequila. I'm not talking about the evil "mixto" liquid you shot in college or the bottom shelf swill you find in crappy dive bar margaritas. Focus on 100% agave tequila. The good stuff. Funky, versatile, and complex, quality tequila is truly one of the world's finest spirits, and your tequila journey begins with a basic understanding of what's inside the bottle.

TEQUILA

Tequila is a spirit derived from the Blue Weber agave, called a "maguey" in Mexico, a succulent related to the aloe plant and technically part of the lily family. It is indigenous to the Tequila region of northwest Mexico, which spans five states, but mostly resides in Jalisco. Agave-based spirits from outside this region or made with another strain of about 200 agave varieties used to be called "mezcals." More on that later. What is fermented and distilled is the agave heart, called the "piña," or "pineapple" (the fruit indeed resembles a giant pineapple). The plant takes 7–12 years to fully mature, and when it does it will weigh between 40 to 75 pounds.

According to Mexican law, only 51% Blue Weber agave is required for a spirit to bear the name "tequila," and those agave blends, usually made with a combination of agave, sugar, or sometimes corn, are called "mixtos." These are to be avoided. Instead, seek out tequilas that are labeled "100% agave" on the label. Consider that your starting point.

The four primary styles of tequila are categorized by the liquid's level of maturation: silver (blanco), reposado, añejo, and extra añejo. Silver tequila is unaged or minimally aged and is clear in color. A decent bottle can be bought for under $30, and an exceptional bottle for less than $50. Lightly aged or age-blended tequila is sometimes referred to as "joven," meaning "young." Reposado ("restful") is aged from two months to 364 days in ex-bourbon barrels or, to a lesser extent, French oak. The barrel imparts a hint of color and infuses subtle notes of vanilla, caramel, and spice from the charred wood to accent the flavors of the agave. Añejo ("old") tequila is aged from one to three years and takes on a deeper amber hue. The spicy, raw nature of the agave relaxes and a stronger cask influence emerges. Tequila aged over three years is called extra añejo and picks up even more wood influence, to the point that producers need to mind that the tannins in the oak don't take over. Extra añejo tequila is best sipped neat.

Tequila is deeply rooted in its terroir, and the region is divided into two main subregions: the highlands (mountains) and the valley of Tequila, referred to as lowlands, which is a misnomer since these valley floors are 4,000 feet above sea level. The highlands, called Los Altos, are 6,000 feet above sea level and dominated by the Sierra Madre del Sur and the Sierra Madre Occidental, which produce a mineral-rich soil, lending a beautiful salinity to highland agave's signature sweet, fruit, and floral-driven notes.

A volcanic range, stretching east to west across Tequila, has created a lava-rich valley floor, producing a smaller agave that imparts herbaceous and earthy notes. When it comes to exploring these subtleties, buyer beware: not all tequilas are created equal. There's a vast commodity market for agave, and many producers aren't so choosy about which subregion the fruit is from, as long as they get the best price. This doesn't make a tequila bad, but it does make it impossible to explore the true expression of its terroir. The solution is estate-grown agave, meaning that the producer controls its own farms. A few estate-grown valley tequilas include Casa Noble, Tequila Fortaleza, and the widely available Herradura, Tapatio, and Ocho.

HOW TO FIND A GOOD TEQUILA

When it comes to finding a good tequila at a decent value, consumers face a minefield of marketing ploys. If a price on a 100% agave tequila seems too good to be true, it probably is. Producers have many tactics to distill their products "efficiently," which affects quality, so don't always believe the hype. Harvesting green agave, employing industrial distilling methods, and adding up to 1% total weight of color and sugar to the mix are a few ways to cut cost and hedge a little flavor.

Then there's the question of where a tequila is made. With around 2,000 brands, there are under 200 operating distilleries in Mexico, so obviously, multiple contracted products are made in large, industrial distilleries. To find out where any tequila is made, look for the Norma Oficial Mexicana (NOM) on the label. The NOM stamp is a guarantee that the bottle's contents meet Mexico's regulatory Tequila requirements. Google any NOM, which is a 4-digit number found on every bottle of tequila, to discover where it is distilled.

NOM 1104

At the end of the day, beginners should find bottles that taste good at a price they are comfortable with, figure out some go-to bottles, and branch out from there. Once you get past the idea of mixtos and focus on real agave, going beyond the hyper-marketed big-box operations like Casa Amigo, Hornitos, or Cuervo's 1800 is a matter of knowing how a product is put together. When I look for a tequila, there are some boxes I like to check, and with some great tequilas I can check most of them: traditional distillation, estate-grown agave, no added color or sugar, reasonable price, family tradition.

① HERRADURA

This is an estate-grown, lowland tequila that is steeped in tradition and boasts a laundry list of innovations and firsts, such as making the first reposado in 1974 and hiring Teresa Lara López, the first female master tequila distiller. Herradura has been traditionally distilling gorgeous tequila since 1870 and never stopped making 100% agave tequila while everyone else resorted to mixto.

② SIETE LEGUAS

When confronted with an extravagantly priced tequila, this is the tequila I measure it against. This pristine distillery makes traditional, tahona wheel (a giant stone wheel that crushes cooked agave to extract juices for distillation), highland tequila in small batches from estate-grown, mature agave to make this naturally sweet, lovely nectar. "So what," I ask, "does your pricey tequila have that Siete does not?" Rarely is there an answer.

③ EL TESORO

El Tesoro is made by tequila legend Carlos Camarena at his fabled La Alteña distillery in the Jalisco highlands, where he grows his agave at least eight years before harvest. His old-school production process takes two weeks, as opposed to an "efficient" tequila, which can be made in just a few days. Camarena also is a leading advocate for environmental initiatives in the region, another great reason to support his fine tequilas.

④ FORTALEZA

Sauza Tequila is best known for its mass-market mixtos, but the Sauza family sold the company a long time ago. Meanwhile, fifth-generation Guillermo Sauza has been making Fortaleza since acquiring an ex-Sauza plant from his grandfather and devoting his life to traditional tequila that is made with a tahona wheel.

⑤ CASA NOBLE

This tequila is made from ripe, estate-grown, lowland organic agaves that are cooked in a stone oven, and it is naturally fermented. But it's the French limousine oak aging that makes Casa Noble stand out. While their blanco is peppery and delicious, there is nothing quite like Casa Noble's reposado or añejo, not to mention their limited, single-barrel extra añejo expressions. If you ever visit the Tequila region, do not miss visiting this beautiful distillery.

PALOMA

What You'll Need:

1.5 oz. 100% agave tequila
1.5 oz. fresh grapefruit juice
1/2 oz. fresh lime juice
1/2 oz. agave syrup
club soda

How to Make It:

Fill a shaker halfway with ice and combine all ingredients except for club soda. Shake until very cold and strain into a highball glass over fresh ice. Top with club soda. Garnish with half a grapefruit wheel and lime.

MEZCAL

If tequila is the well-groomed member of the agave family, its mysterious, Oaxacan cousin, Mezcal, is a bit of a hippie: funky, a little strange, and occasionally smelling like smoke. This is why you should be drinking it.

Back in the day, mezcal was merely a spirit distilled from the fermentation of sugars derived from any variety of maguey. All distilled agave spirits used to fall under this banner, including tequila. Then in 1995, the Mexican government declared the term "mezcal" a denomination of origin (Tequila became a DO in 1978)—and what was a broad category of spirit became a terroir-driven, self-contained product hailing primarily from Oaxaca and mostly distilled with the Espadín agave. Like the Blue Weber, Espadín is a farmable, sustainable strain that can be grown to scale.

But unlike tequila, mezcal is not restricted to one strain of agave, so its flavors fall all over the map. Throw in some ancient and, ahem, unconventional distilling techniques, like employing insects, nuts, honey, or even a chicken breast, called a *pechuga mezcal*, into the distillate to find your flavor profile and you have one of the world's most unique, unpredictable tasting spirits whose flavors are rooted in individualism and personality. In fact, while the market is festooned with industrially made tequila hiding in old-school packaging, mezcal has always been predominantly artisanal. Predictably, as its popularity grows, things are beginning to change, so finding a good bottle can be tricky.

HOW TO FIND A GOOD MEZCAL

Rule Out Industrial Mezcal: Today's mezcal on the modern back bar generally falls into three camps: industrial, artisanal, and ancestral. Finding these words on the label is an excellent place to begin. "Artisanal" mezcal is a broad term that assures the drinker the spirit was produced with a minimum standard of traditional methods. Ancestral is the rarest and most cherished mezcal. By law ancestral mezcal must be fermented in a natural container, like clay, wood, or animal skin. Piñas must be crushed without a mechanical shredder. The traditional method is a mule-drawn tahona wheel, and the spirit is distilled in a clay pot still. Unless you know what you are looking for, the absence of the words "artisanal" and "ancestral" increases the likelihood that you are getting an industrially made product that should be avoided.

Look Past Age Statements: Like tequila, many mezcals are aged and labeled "reposado" and "añejo." I have no beef with these; Illegal Mezcal makes some killer reposado mezcal. But the fact is, traditional mezcal is drunk unaged, making joven or blanco the best way to explore the true expression of that agave.

Clear Up the Smoke: Ancient mezcal distillation involved roasting the agave in earthen pits, which imparts deep smoky flavors, and most commercial producers incorporate these smoky characteristics into their mezcals. But many fine sipping mezcals are not smoky at all, as smoke covers the delicate terroir-driven flavors of agave.

Size Matters: To get a sense of how big a mezcal is, look for batch size. No matter how strict the rules, large producers will always find a way to make themselves look small, but one piece of information they cannot circumvent is the batch size. Few producers will label a batch size at 5,000 liters since this tells the drinker there is no way the product was made artisanally. Many small producers will include a batch of 500 liters, which means there is a much higher likelihood that you are getting a traditionally made mezcal.

Not All Artisanal Mezcals Are Created Equally, and That's OK: As a rule, you will find that the smoky, less expensive artisanal mezcals, like Del Maguey Vida or Sombra, are uniform, affordable, and built for cocktails. They're starter mezcals, if you will, and not terroir-driven. But they make damn good margaritas.

Artisinal or Ancestral Doesn't Always Taste Good: You might find a beautiful bottle of small-batch mezcal made in tiny quantities and distilled in the strictest adherence to traditional methods—and it still might suck. Remember the rule: only drink what tastes good to you.

MEZCAL MULE

I make this margarita for customers in my bar who are interested in mezcal but balk at dropping $16 on a cocktail they're afraid they'll hate. A mezcal rinse on a tequila-based margarita lends a whiff of smoke and a beautiful layer of complexity that never overwhelms the drink. But for the committed, my go-to is this killer spin on the Moscow mule, which in my opinion blows the vodka-based classic away.

MEZCAL MULE

What You'll Need:
1.5 oz. mezcal
1/2 oz. fresh lime juice
ginger beer

How to Make It: Fill a mule mug (if unavailable, use a rocks glass) with ice. Add mezcal and fresh lime. Top with ginger beer and stir. Garnish with a lime wheel and mint leaf.

GIN: THE ULTIMATE COCKTAILER

It took me a long time to warm up to gin. It was one of the first liquors I ever tried as a kid, and I must say, I was appalled by it. I could not get past its "pine tree" flavor, which comes from the juniper berry, gin's dominant botanical. But gin and I have long since come to an understanding: if it stays in a cocktail, we can be friends. Over the years, we have grown to become better friends than I care to admit. This chameleon of a spirit never fails to make its presence known, adding layers of complexity to drinks and blending beautifully with fruit juices, citrus, liqueurs, and Champagne. There is even scientific evidence proving that gin's juniper and tonic's quinine make each other taste better. But gin and tonics alone are hardly responsible for the gin revolution that is currently raging right before our eyes.

Gin's signature note is juniper, which serves as the cornerstone for its crisp, clean, iconic flavor and is the lead botanical in a list of seven classics used to create the spirit: anise, angelica root, cinnamon, orange peel, coriander, and cassia bark round out the roster. In Merry Old England back in the 18th and 19th centuries, "Old Tom" style gin was the toast of the town, but it wasn't always the finest crafted spirit. These gins of yore were commonly crudely distilled rotgut doctored by shady purveyors with nasty additives that they doused with botanicals and sugars to mask the off flavors. The hangovers must have been brutal. The invention of the column still in 1938 allowed distillate to be produced cleaner and more efficiently, and as the quality of gin's base spirit improved, unsweetened "dry" gins steadily gained popularity and eventually replaced the Old Tom style. Most of these dry gins were being made in London at the time, hence the name: London Dry.

Over two centuries later, the winds of change are blowing as modern distillers are writing the next chapter in gin's storied history by distilling "new school" gins featuring out-of-the-box botanicals designed to share the spotlight with the expected juniper (which must be present for the spirit to be considered a gin) and less neutral distillates. Hendrick's is a household name gin whose cucumber and rose-forward profile tempers the sharp bite of juniper, making the gin more approachable and thereby attracting a new flock of gin devotees.

While the purists predictably cry blasphemy at the irreverence to their beloved juniper, clever bartenders are breaking down barriers with nuanced flavor profiling in cocktails. The mixology scene's current obsession with old-school, pre-Prohibition classics has revived interest in the tried-and-true gin classics like Old Tom, London Dry, and the very first gin of them all, Dutch genever. Here are a few traditional stalwarts and contemporary brands to explore.

OLD WORLD CLASSICS

① **BEEFEATER**

Named after the Tower of London's Yeoman Warders, Beefeater is the benchmark against which all other London Dry is measured. Beefeater's recipe of classic botanicals has remained virtually unchanged since its inception in the 1860s, and the brand is world famous for its in-your-face juniper with a supporting cast of citrus and herbs. Try it in a martini—see page 70.

② **BOMBAY SAPPHIRE**

Bombay Sapphire came to be in 1987, and while it doesn't claim the history others might boast, the brand quickly emerged as a contemporary, classic, bone-dry gin.

③ **TANQUERAY**

A hit of fresh grapefruit is the perfect foil in a creamy yet bone-dry Tanqueray G&T, or learn the simple, sexy classic Bee's Knees, which calls for a sharp London Dry to pierce through its lemon and honey flavors.

BEE'S KNEES

What You'll Need:
2 oz. London dry gin
3/4 oz. fresh lemon juice
1/2 oz. honey syrup

How to Make It: To make the honey syrup, combine honey and hot water in a container and stir until completely mixed.
In a shaker tin, combine fresh lemon juice, honey syrup, gin, and ice. Shake vigorously and strain into a coupe glass.

HOW TO MAKE A LONDON DRY

For a gin to be "London Dry," the base spirit must be neutral, meaning alcohol must be distilled to at least 96%, which strips the flavor, leaving a clean, virtually tasteless and odorless "neutral spirit." This is also how vodka is made. The botanicals are added to the spirit through one of two standard methods: distilled and redistilled. Distilled gin's botanicals are added during the original distillation, while a gin like Beefeater is typically made with purchased, off-the-market, neutral spirit that is then redistilled with the botanical recipe. One thing a London Dry gin does not need to be is from London. The term was developed to protect its production methods, not its place of origin.

NEW-SCHOOL COOL

COPPER & KINGS AMERICAN DRY

Citrus peel and lavender are the dominant notes alongside juniper in C&K's American Dry Gin. But it's not the botanicals that set it apart, it's the distillate. Made from pressed apples and twice distilled in alembic pot stills to retain flavor, the brandy-style base spirit is about as far from "neutral" as you can get. Try this new-school American craft in a Corpse Reviver 2, which is a 1930's spinoff of the pre-Prohibition, brandy-based Corpse Reviver, for a unique cocktail that nods to both.

CORPSE REVIVER 2

What You'll Need:
1 1/2 oz absinthe
3/4 oz Copper & Kings American Dry
3/4 oz Cointreau
3/4 oz Lillet Blanc
3/4 oz fresh lemon juice

How to Make It: Rinse a chilled cocktail or coupe glass with absinthe. Add remaining ingredients into a shaker, fill halfway with ice, and shake until cold. Strain and serve straight up.

AVIATION

Oregon-based Aviation's signature botanical of lavender sits atop a malty, spicy rye base that sets this craft gin pioneer apart from traditional London Dry. In fact, Aviation deemed themselves "New Western Dry," a movement still searching for its voice. Try it in a French 75. The lavender notes and soft Indian sarsaparilla spice mesh beautifully with crisp sparkling wine and fresh lemon, and it makes an impressive date-night opener to a meal.

FRENCH 75

What You'll Need:
1/2 oz. fresh lemon juice
1/2 oz. simple syrup
1 oz. Aviation Gin
3 oz. dry sparkling wine

How to Make It: Add gin, lemon juice, and simple syrup into a shaker. Add ice and shake until very cold. Strain into a Champagne flute and top with dry sparkling wine. Garnish with a lemon twist.

THE BOTANIST

The Botanist is made at the Bruichladdich distillery in Islay, Scotland, and contains 22 locally sourced botanicals that combine to impart peppery and spicy flavors, the makings of a mind-bending eye opener—the Red Snapper, a Bloody Mary made with gin.

RED SNAPPER

What You'll Need:

2 oz gin

4 oz tomato juice

1/2 oz freshly squeezed lemon juice

4–5 dashes Worcestershire sauce

1 teaspoon horseradish

Tabasco to taste

pinch celery salt

2 pinches black pepper

How to Make It: Combine ingredients into a shaker. Fill halfway with ice and shake until cold. Strain into a highball glass and garnish with a celery stalk and lime wedge.

RUM'S THE WORD

A rum fantasy: It's late at night on the open sea. A ship comes into view through the murky darkness, helmed by a famous pirate sea captain who's synonymous with a certain spiced rum. Suddenly another boat approaches, and the captain is taken by surprise. Boarded, raided, and sacked, the ship's men are tied up, their women taken, and their galleys and hulls picked clean. As the pirate thieves sail back into the abyss with their booty, the only thing left behind is the captain's crappy rum. The moral of the story? You can drink better.

Artificially flavored stuff aside, rum is arguably the most underrated spirit. It's a complex chameleon that runs from light, crispy cocktailers to beautifully aged slow sippers that are every bit as decadent as a fine cognac (sorry, France) and pairs impeccably with a good cigar.

Almost all of the rums we drink, aged or otherwise, are made from molasses, a syrupy sugarcane by-product steeped in dubious history involving the Caribbean's slave-driven sugar trade in the mid-17th century. The first known rum in the States was distilled on Staten Island around 1670. "Kill-devil," or "rumbullion," became the colonies' spirit of choice throughout colonial times. It's believed Paul Revere stopped for a snort on his way to warn the Revolutionary army that "the British are coming." And when the British came, they were probably packing flasks themselves. The British Royal Navy gave rum rations, called "tot," to its soldiers for 300 years. The practice was abolished on July 31, 1970, a day known as Black Tot Day in England.

These days, a persistent rumor is that aged rum is in line to become the next spirit to experience a spike in popularity like bourbon did ten years ago. It's a refrain I've been hearing for years, and that shoe has yet to drop. That's not to say rum is a sleepy category, though. Today's sales hover around $2 billion per year. That's a lot of Captain and Cokes.

Rum is made all over the world. Asia, Africa, the Caribbean, the Americas, and Europe are all producers, leading to incredible displays of flavors, aromas, and styles. The downside is that this diversity also makes rum a little confusing to follow. Not all French "rhum" is "agricole," and not all Spanish "ron" is built for cocktails. The rules of how rum can be produced vary from one country to the next. Meanwhile, rums of different styles are routinely blended, making it virtually impossible to fit the category into tidy boxes. But I am going to do it anyway.

At their essence, the rums we enjoy are based on three distinct styles: Spanish, English, and French. These are the building blocks for what will hopefully be a life-changing journey into this beautiful and often misunderstood spirit.

LATIN-STYLE RUM

This is the light, dry, "party in a glass" that's the trademark of traditional rums from the islands of Puerto Rico, Cuba, and the Dominican Republic. Molasses undergoes a short fermentation period, then is column or multiple-column distilled at a high proof, resulting in a clean distillate that is either bottled unaged, young, or matured in a barrel for decades. These rums are made to be consumed by the people of these islands, and the culture is all about mixed drinks. But these Latin-style rums also age beautifully and adapt notes of vanilla, caramel, fruits, and spices from ex-bourbon barrels, the predominant cask for rum aging. So whether you are looking for your favorite base for a daiquiri, mojito, or Cuba libre (a fancy name for a rum and coke), or you are exploring fine sippers, here are a few classics that will take you beyond Bacardi, Malibu, and the Captain.

① CRUZAN

Even though what's now Beam Suntory purchased Cruzan in 2008, the Nelthropp family have run this US Virgin Islands–based rum for six generations. President Gary Nelthropp describes Cruzan as "the clean rum," with a five-column distillation process that cranks the rum's proof up to 189.6, just a cut below a vodka—making this a good starter rum for vodka drinkers.

② DON Q

While Bacardi is by far the world's largest selling rum, the people of Puerto Rico are partial to Don Q, which is a textbook example of traditional Spanish style. To produce their signature Don Q Cristal, sixth-generation master distiller Roberto Serrallés employs multiple-column stills to provide a clean and dry distillate that ages in a barrel for one year, per Puerto Rican law. The color is charcoal filtered out for that "cristal" clean look. For a finely aged rum, go for Don Q Grand Anejo, which is a blend of rums aged between 9 and 12 years.

③ BRUGAL

The Dominican Republic's biggest rum brand is Brugal, first distilled in 1920 and brought to the United States in 1981. Brugal's entry-level Blanco Supremo is aged between two and five years, putting a surprising dose of chocolate, vanilla, and coffee bean flavors into a bright spirit whose color, like Don Q's, is filtered out. The company's top-of-the-line blend of multi-cask aged and beautifully blended rum is Papa Andres, a limited release of which only about a thousand are made available.

MOJITO

To make an authentic mojito, you need to use cane sugar and build it in the glass. Also, the empty lime hull ends up in the drink. I prefer this somewhat easier but tasty recipe when cranking out mojitos. After all, when do you only make one Mojito? Nobody complains that it's not the real thing.

MOJITO

What You'll Need:
3/4 oz. simple syrup
2 sprigs mint, plus more for garnish
2 oz. rum
3/4 oz. fresh lime juice
club soda (for serving)

How to Make It: Gently muddle simple syrup and mint sprigs in a cocktail shaker. Add rum and lime juice. Fill shaker with ice, cover, and shake vigorously until outside of shaker is very cold, about 20 seconds. Strain through a Hawthorne strainer or slotted spoon into a tall collins glass filled with ice. Top off with club soda. Garnish with extra mint.

ENGLISH RUM

Old-world Caribbean rums of Jamaica and Barbados, known as the birthplace of modern rum, are produced in traditional pot stills, yielding a viscous, full-bodied rum that is the trademark of the English style. These are big, bold rums that burst with flavors and aromas and, when made well, age beautifully, even in the hot Caribbean sun. Here are some classics.

APPLETON ESTATE

Nestled into the sugarcane fields from which their rum is fermented, bottled, and distilled, Appleton Estate's 265-year-old distillery is the oldest working distillery in Jamaica. Either pot- or pot-and-column stilled, Jamaica's most famous rum is produced under the watchful eye of master blender Joyce Spence, the first female to be given the title. The entry-level rum is Appleton Signature Blend, a combination of 15 different styles of rums whose age averages 4 years, but the age-stated 12-year-old blend is where it's at. Appleton 21-year-old is a very special rum if you can find it. I've got a bottle stashed away for a special occasion.

PUSSER'S NAVAL RUM

The story goes like this: when the British navy's daily tot was doled out by "pussers," sailors would ignite the rum, which would burn at "proof," which is 54.5% ABV. And woe was the pusser to fail this test. Pusser's "Gunpowder Proof" claims to employ the blending recipe last used by the Royal Navy in 1970, and since it is 109 proof, it will probably light on fire. But the viscous 15-year-old from Guyana is laden with dried-fruit flavors, representing the best in the line. I'd love to get my hands on a bottle of Pusser's 150 proof Naval Rum, but it's only available in Germany.

FOUR SQUARE

Rock star distiller Richard Seale's rum serves as a base for rum brands including Red Harbor Doorlys, Rum 66, Old Brigand, R.L. Seale, Tommy Bahama, and Real McCoy at his Four Square Distillery in Barbados. But Seale's elusive Four Square rum is often considered the Pappy Van Winkle of rum, though it's a lot less expensive. All Four Square rums are free of added sugar, liquid tannin, or other little tricks of the trade. Seale's coveted single-blended rums are aged in ex-bourbon barrels and, in the case of the 2006 vintage, cognac barrels. This cask-strength rum is considered one of the gold standard rums being produced today.

FRENCH RHUM AGRICOLE

French-born rhum agricole is made from pressed sugarcane in place of molasses and represents the classic French style from the islands of Martinique, Guyana, and Guadeloupe. Today, the agricole style is distilled all over the Caribbean and South America, and craft distillers are beginning to produce agricultural sugarcane rums here in the States. Grassy, herbal, slightly vegetal, and a little bit funky, rhum agricoles make for a sophisticated, terroir-driven sipper and interesting, exotic cocktails whose very presence on a menu screams sophistication.

CLÉMENT V.S.O.P. RHUM AGRICOLE

Distilled in the Habitation Clément distillery in Martinique, this is a quintessential rhum agricole that complies with the island's strict guidelines dictating the rhum's production. Sugarcane must be crushed and fermented within 24 hours of pressing. It must use fresh sugarcane juice, and it is required that white rhum be unaged. Aged rhums are matured in French oak cognac barrels, in this case, a minimum of four years. While unaged rhum agricole is grassy and herbaceous with a sugarcane nose and a dry finish, aged agricoles take on fruit and gentle spice and a hint of smoke from the barrel, which becomes more prevalent as the rhum matures.

CLAIRIN

Meanwhile, rhum agricole's close cousin, Clairin, is a spirit few know about, which naturally makes it cool. While Barbancourt is the best-known Haitian rum (it's good) and it's made from cane, it's really not a rhum agricole. But you will come close with Clairins Rhum Pur Jus De Canne. Clairins is a local spirit in the Haitian hills that is made from chemical-free cane that's naturally fermented (meaning no commercial yeast is added) in distilleries called guildives, a Hatian spin on kill-devil. There are about 500 guildives in Haiti, most of them barely make enough rhum to supply the town in which the distiller lives. This local style represents some of the most traditional and "authentic" spirits commercially available, and clairins is usually single-distilled in pot stills and bottled raw and unfiltered. Every bottling has its own style, and each is named after either the distiller or the distillery. Labels are often colorfully designed by local artists. Earthy, grassy, and distinctly funkier than the rums of Martinique and Guadeloupe, people either love Clairins or hate it. To discover which camp you fall in, you need to seek it out.

LA MAISON AND VELIER

These importers bring four clairin expressions to the United States, each offering up its own vibe, and they taste vastly different from each other. Clairin Communal is a blend of clairin from different guildives; Casimir comes from the Distillerie Faubert Casimir, Barraderes, Haiti; Clarins Sajous is produced by local legend Michael Sajous; and Clarin Vaval, another single estate, is from the Distillerie Arawaks, Cavaillon, Haiti.

PETIT PUNCH

This simple punch recipe was given to me by the infamous
Jeff "Beachbum" Berry. It's not only perfect for a crowd, but
it's the official cocktail of Martinique. The drink is ideal in
its simplicity; the spirit is complex so you don't want big
flavors to compete. Just a balanced backdrop is all you
need to allow the spirit to shine through.

PETIT PUNCH

What You'll Need:
2 oz. of unaged rhum agricole
1/4 oz. fresh lime juice (about a
wedge's worth)
1 tsp. simple syrup
lime wedge

How to Make It: Add all ingredients
in a highball glass filled with ice, and
stir. Garnish with lime wedge.

SEVEN COCKTAILS EVERY GENTLEMAN SHOULD KNOW

Any common cave-dweller can fuel an evening with ye olde 12-pack, but the refined gentleman doesn't roll that way. When it comes to hosting, what you serve your friends and family defines you. The ability to create delicious, memorable cocktails—signature drinks around which a party swirls— separates the mediocre from guys with the ability to entertain, impress, and indulge in incredible libations for the rest of one's days. Be that guy.

Chances are you're already a bartender, even if you aren't good at it. I certainly wasn't. It was a dark time for cocktails before the mixology scene gained momentum in New York City a decade ago. The idea of creating refined concoctions crafted to showcase, but not overpower, the qualities of carefully curated spirits wasn't a thing; nobody was Instagramming their Chocolate Negronis. Cocktails with friends meant drowning cheap booze in sugary juice or soda. You knew going in that the next day was going to hurt. Primitive as it was, we were still making drinks—highballs as it turns out—and eventually things evolved. Sloppy rum and colas gave way to clean, hydrating tequila and sodas, slick martinis, and tart, spicy margaritas—a world of deliciousness from which you'll never go back.

The fundamentals of balancing spirit, sour (acidity), bitter, and sweet is the cornerstone of what makes a drink taste good, and building the skills to produce quality drinks begins with mastering the classics. The seven quintessential cocktails in this chapter form the foundation of modern mixology, and learning them is key to a lifetime of drinking well. All it takes is a handful of bar tools, a few key ingredients, and practice, practice, practice. But hey, that's the best part.

HOME BAR ESSENTIALS: THE BASICS

Raising your mixology game requires a bit of preparation, and you'll need a few tools to establish a basic home bar. There's no need to buy expensive stuff, though. Instead, invest in decent quality barware, and like all tools, keep them clean and well-maintained and they should last. Cocktailkingdom.com or Thecraftybartender.com are useful resources.

BAR TOOLS

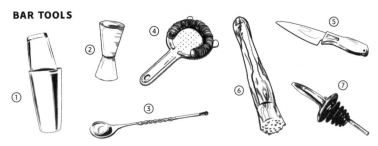

① **Boston shaker:** The quintessential vessel in which to build your cocktail. Pick up small, medium, and large shakers, using the large for multiple drinks and the small and medium for single cocktails.

② **Jigger:** Master mixologists measure their alcohol to assure balance and consistency. Start with 1 oz. and 2 oz. jiggers with 1/4 oz. incremental markings on the inside.

③ **Bar spoon:** Doling out teaspoons and cracking ice are a few uses of this versatile bar tool, but its long-handled swizzle is instrumental in stirring Manhattans, Negronis, and martinis. Not to mention fishing out floaties.

④ **Hawthorne strainer:** This strainer sits atop a shaker to pour out your drinks. Pop the coil inside the perimeter of the shaker, then push the strainer forward and pour.

⑤ **Bar knife:** Instrumental in cutting fruit and slicing a twist of orange or lemon. You don't need anything fancy here, just as long as your knife is sharp. I prefer a serrated blade, but that's your call. Kuhn Rikon makes an inexpensive, highly effective, reliable bar blade for about $10.

⑥ **Muddler:** Smash, macerate, and crush herbs, fruits, and other ingredients with this cool tool. Sure, you can use a wooden spoon, but a solid muddler does a superior job.

⑦ **Speed pour:** This may seem fussy, but it's easier to nail exact measurements in a jigger with this tool. The more you practice, the easier it becomes to control your pour.

GLASSWARE

Placing a beautifully crafted cocktail in an inferior vessel is inexcusable. These three styles of appropriate glassware make most cocktails look presentable:

① **Cocktail glass:** Try a 6-ouncer so your 4-oz. martini has a little breathing room.

② **Rocks/old-fashioned glass:** Cut glass or clear, it's your call. Always seek out a rocks glass that feels good in your hand and holds about 6–8 oz. of liquid.

③ **Highball/collins glass:** Size matters here. A tall, slender 10–12 oz. glass looks classy and will accommodate most cocktails nicely.

SEVEN QUINTESSENTIAL COCKTAILS

THE MARTINI

A martini is a fancy glass of chilled gin or vodka, dry vermouth, and a garnish. Yep, that's it. But that doesn't mean making one is a slam dunk. The secret to a killer martini is making it extremely cold without over-diluting, which is why stirring is preferred to shaking, regardless of how James Bond likes his. From there, it's all a matter of style. Martini styles range from an old-timey recipe of 1:1 to a "bone dry" cocktail with barely a whisper of vermouth. Today's standard martini is 3:1, but feel free to experiment to find your sweet spot. Raise your game with blue cheese hand-stuffed olives. They take only a few minutes to prepare and blow away most pre-made brands. Just jam "queen" pitted olives full of quality blue cheese or gorgonzola. Skewer, and drop into your martini for a decadent upgrade.

THE MARTINI

What You'll Need:
3 oz. gin or vodka
1 oz. dry vermouth

How to Make It: Add ingredients and ice to shaker and stir until very cold, about 30 seconds. Strain straight up in a chilled martini glass. Garnish with olives or a lemon twist and serve.

Riffing on the Classic

· **Dirty:** Replace 1/2 oz. spirit with olive juice. Filthy? Amp it up to 3/4 oz.
· **Espresso:** Combine 2 oz. vodka with 1 oz. espresso and 1 oz. Kahlua. Shake. Strain up in a martini glass and garnish with 3 espresso beans.

- **Berry**: In a shaker, muddle 2 raspberries, 1 blackberry, half a strawberry, or the equivalent. Add 3 oz. spirit, 1/2 oz. syrup, and 1/2 oz. lemon juice. Shake and fine strain straight up in a martini glass.
- **Gibson:** Swap out the olives or peel for cocktail onions.

BURNING QUESTION: HOW DO BARTENDERS MAKE THOSE THIN, SWIRLY TWISTS?

A channel knife is a tool that will help you pull off a loopy, elegant-looking twist that looks slick in a martini. Just catch the blade under the skin and firmly twist around a lemon peel. Wrap around your finger for a nice curl. For an old fashioned or a Negroni, go for a thicker twist (a peeler does a fabulous job), or practice getting a thin peel with as little white pith as possible with your knife.

CLASSIC MANHATTAN

The best Manhattan is made with ingredients that you like, not the preference of some swirly-mustachioed mixologist. So, if you prefer a caramel-laden bourbon to a spicy, fruity rye, put that in your cocktail. Experimenting with different Italian or sweet vermouths will also help hone your personal style. Be sure to garnish with a quality brandied cherry, not a syrupy, neon maraschino. Pro tip: Remember New York City's area code, 2-1-2, and you won't forget the Manhattan's measurements: 2 oz. rye, 1 oz. vermouth, 2 dashes bitters.

Riffing on the Classic

· **Dry:** Replace sweet Italian vermouth with dry French vermouth.
· **Perfect:** Replace 1 oz. sweet vermouth with 1/2 oz. sweet and 1/2 oz. dry vermouth.
· **Black:** Swap out vermouth for Averna, a bittersweet Italian digestif. Go with a 3:1 or 4:1 ratio of whiskey to liqueur to suit your taste.

CLASSIC MANHATTAN

What You'll Need:

2 oz. rye whiskey

1 oz. sweet vermouth, such as Antica Formula or Cocchi Storico Vermouth di Torino

2 dashes Angostura bitters

How to Make It: Fill a shaker halfway with ice. Add ingredients and stir until extremely cold, about 30 seconds. Strain straight up in a chilled martini glass. Garnish with brandied cherries.

BURNING QUESTION: WHAT EXACTLY IS VERMOUTH?

Vermouth is an aromatized, fortified wine that has been spiked with alcohol (brandy) and a recipe of herbs, bitters, citrus, and spices. Vermouth was invented in Italy in the 18th century, yet its name was derived from the German word *wermut*, which translates to "wormwood," a bitter aromatic that is also used to flavor absinthe. The two most common varieties are Italian sweet vermouth, used in Manhattans, and dry French vermouth, favored in martinis.

OLD FASHIONED

Back in the 19th century, a "cocktail" was a specific drink, just like a collins, flip, or rickey, and had five ingredients: a base spirit, bitters, sugar, water (or ice), and peel. It was after Prohibition when "cocktail" evolved into a generic term for any mixed drink. So, to get the real thing, you would request an "old fashioned" whiskey cocktail. The name stuck. This classic recipe calls for the traditional method of muddling a sugar cube in a rocks glass and dissolving it with a touch of club soda. Pro tip: When mixing for a crowd, it's cool to build it in a shaker and use 1/2 oz. of simple syrup to quickly crank out drinks.

Riffing on the Classic

· **Gin Old Fashioned:** Pull back on the sugar (1/4 oz.) and use a few dashes of orange bitters in place of Angostura with your favorite gin for a refreshing botanical-based sipper.

• **Oaxaca Old Fashioned:** Replace whiskey with smoky mezcal, then swap out the Angostura bitters for a molé or chocolate variety if you choose to seek them out. More readily available orange bitters work nicely as well.

• **Apple Brandy Old Fashioned:** Swap out whiskey for apple brandy and go with 1/2 oz. maple syrup instead of sugar. Two dashes of Angostura bitters and a peel. Just like the classic.

OLD FASHIONED

What You'll Need:

2 oz. rye or bourbon
1 sugar cube (preferably demerara, but white sugar cubes work)
club soda
2 dashes Angostura bitters
2 dashes orange bitters
orange or lemon peel

How to Make It: In a rocks glass, add sugar, a splash of club soda, and bitters. Muddle into a thick slurry. Add whiskey and a king cube or a few chunks of ice, and stir until cold. Twist orange peel to release the oils, rub the rim of the glass, and drop into drink.

BURNING QUESTION: WHAT THE HELL ARE BITTERS?

Considered the salt and pepper of bartending, bitters are concentrated flavoring agents made with high proof alcohol and a recipe of botanicals to add depth, seasoning, and complexity to cocktails. Trinidad's classic Angostura remains a staple in any bar, but Fee Brothers, Peychaud's, and Regan's are a few of many great brands worth checking out.

DAIQUIRI

Forget about any conceptions of this cocktail as a floofy umbrella drink, a connotation that was well earned during the frozen strawberry daiquiri craze in the '80s. Instead, get hip to this textbook recipe of 2 oz. base spirit and 3/4 oz. each sugar and citrus—a template that serves as the bones for cocktails all over the world. This one is a Spanish-style daiquiri with fresh lime and sugar, shaken and strained over cracked ice; it's a simple, refreshing Cuban quaff that any home bartender can pull off. To crack large cubes, place them in a towel and whack them with the back of your bar spoon.

Riffing on the Classic

For a real frozen strawberry daiquiri, add 1 strawberry and a 1/4 cup of cracked ice in a blender. You can take it from there.

DAIQUIRI

What You'll Need:
2 oz. rum
3/4 oz. lime juice
3/4 oz. simple syrup

How to Make It: Fill a shaker halfway with ice. Add lime juice, sugar, and rum. Shake until the shaker is very cold in your hand. Strain "up" in a chilled cocktail glass. Garnish with a lime wheel.

BURNING QUESTION: HOW DO BARTENDERS GET THEIR DRINKS TO FROTH?

Egg whites. To add froth without artificial ingredients or adding flavor, separate an egg and place the white in a shaker. Remove the coil from your Hawthorne strainer and "dry shake" the egg white until it turns frothy, about one minute. Add to your cocktail, shake, and pour.

HIGHBALL

There are tons of fussy, carefully balanced cocktails that can be ruined with one false move. That's not this. Originally invented as a whiskey drink, the lines of what makes a highball have long since blurred. A base spirit mixed with soda, accented with garnish, and served over ice is all it takes, and even the garnish is optional. Like any solid cocktail, balance is critical. A 2:1 ratio is the standard measurement here, but if you find a balance that tastes good to you, stick with it. Bonus! Quaffing this highly adaptable cocktail is like having a glass of water with every drink. A little hydration today makes for a far more pleasant tomorrow.

Riffing on the Classic

• **Switch up your garnish:** Don't be afraid to get creative with garnish. Fruits and herbs, like mint or basil, work well, as do lemon and orange peel. A thin, lengthwise slice of cucumber looks sexy and provides a refreshing, subtle pop.

• **Any base spirit is in play:** The highball is a highly adaptable drink in which virtually any base spirit will shine. Gin, vodka, and tequila are all on the table. If it tastes good to you, your spirit of choice is fair game.

· **Add flavors:** While the classic is whiskey and club, any mixed drink of soda and spirit, like gin and tonic (soda + spirit), technically qualifies. For a Tom Collins, combine 2 oz. Old Tom gin with 3/4 lemon and 1/2 oz. simple syrup, and top with club soda over ice. The sky is the limit, so if it tastes good to you, don't let someone tell you that you're doing it wrong.

HIGHBALL

What You'll Need:
3 oz. club soda (quality bubbles like Q or Fever Tree recommended)
1 1/2 oz. whiskey (try a Japanese whiskey like Hakushu 12–Year–Old)
mint leaf for garnish (or herb, peel, or fruit wedge of your choosing)

How to Make It: Combine ingredients in a chilled highball glass filled with cracked ice. Stir, and garnish with a mint leaf.

BURNING QUESTION: WHAT'S THE DIFFERENCE BETWEEN CLUB SODA AND SELTZER WATER?

Short answer? Salt. Seltzer is carbonated water, meaning carbon dioxide has been pumped into H_2O to provide its fizz. Club soda has minerals like sodium bicarbonate, potassium salts, and even table salt added for flavor and to neutralize acidity.

MARGARITA

This tequila cocktail has acquired a bad rap in certain circles. Chain restaurants, mediocre bars, and other Neanderthals have reduced the margarita to a sugary mess of artificial sour mix and bottom shelf hooch. But the real thing is a whole different animal. This simple masterpiece is a balancing act of 100% agave tequila, lime, and triple sec, an orange liqueur—a backdrop of sweet and tart that's punched up with a little salt. A classic margarita is technically a three-ingredient drink, but I like to add a 1/4 oz. of agave syrup to mine.

Riffing on the Classic

· **Spicy Margarita:** Add a centimeter-length slice of jalapeño to shaker. Muddle, and build drink on top. Fine strain to catch any seeds.

· **Blue Margarita:** Sure, curacao is a little kitschy, but there's always room for a cool blue drink, am I right? Just follow the traditional recipe and swap out triple sec with blue curacao for a fun drink that never fails to turn heads.

MARGARITA

What You'll Need:

2 oz. 100% agave silver (blanco) tequila

3/4 oz. triple sec (orange liqueur, Cointreau is a quality brand)

3/4 oz. fresh lime juice

1/4 oz agave syrup (optional)

kosher salt

How to Make It: Rim half the glass with salt. Fill a shaker halfway with ice and add tequila, triple sec, and lime juice. Shake until the shaker is very cold in your hand. Strain over fresh ice in a rocks glass, or try it "up" in a cocktail glass without ice. Garnish with a lime wheel.

· **Strawberry Margarita:** Muddle a small, ripe strawberry (or half a large one) in your shaker and build your margarita on top of it. Shake hard and fine strain. For a raspberry, blackberry, or watermelon version, follow the same procedure with like amounts of fruit.

WHAT'S AN EASY WAY TO SALT A RIM?

Spread kosher salt into a shallow bowl. Moisten half the outside rim of your glass with a lime or orange wedge and roll it in the salt. Try not to get salt in the drink, but a little bit is OK.

NEGRONI

I first ordered the Italian classic in Harry's bar in Florence, and while the alluring, deep ruby hue of this gin-based cocktail appeared sweet and playful, the Negroni's bitter, medicinal bite was more than my palate could reconcile. As I worked my way through the drink, the challenging flavors began making sense, and before my glass was empty, I ordered another.

It's made of equal parts Campari, sweet vermouth, and London dry gin, stirred and backed up with an orange peel. This simple sipper is a sexy, sophisticated signature drink that pleases devotees and challenges the uninitiated.

Riffing on the Classic

About six years ago I worked with Naren Young, now beverage director at Dante in New York, on a cocktail column I used to write called "Happy Hour," and he hooked me up with the recipe for his signature Chocolate Negroni. Recently I read an interview where he spoke about how he's carried this recipe with him for over a decade. And it hasn't changed.

NEGRONI

What You'll Need:

1 oz. gin

1 oz. Campari

1 oz. sweet vermouth

orange peel

How to Make It: Fill a shaker halfway with ice. Combine all ingredients except the peel in a shaker and stir until very cold, about 30 rotations. Strain over fresh ice or a king cube and serve with an orange twist.

CHOCOLATE NEGRONI

What You'll Need:

1 oz. gin

3/4 oz. Campari

3/4 oz. Punt e Mes

2 dashes chocolate bitters

1/4 oz. white crème de cacao

orange twist (for garnish)

How to Make It: Half-fill a mixing glass with ice. Add the ingredients, stir, and strain into a cocktail glass. Garnish with the orange twist.

BURNING QUESTION: WHAT THE HELL IS THE DEAL WITH KING CUBES?

King cubes are large square ice cubes, usually about 2", whose large surface area makes the ice melt slowly, hence chilling your drink instead of watering it down. Molds are readily available.

PARTY TIME!

When it comes to entertaining, friends in my world have come to expect something special when I am taking care of drinks, whether it's a cocktail for one or a tailgate for twenty. Creating memorable experiences has been a priority throughout my adult life, and I have learned that the simple act of placing a beautifully made cocktail in a friend's hand is a powerful gesture. The key to effortless entertaining with killer cocktails is preparation: make drinks ahead of time in scalable batches. Here are a few recipes I've collected from great mixologists.

SPRING: TAILGATERS BOURBON BUCK

There are two John McCarthys in the spirits game: me and Johnny Mac, a talented mixologist and coauthor of *Be Your Own Bartender*, which he wrote with his wife, journalist Carey Jones. For years we have received each other's emails, invites, and liquor samples. Once a liquor company offered to hire me to bartend a private event long before I learned how to shake. I told them I would do it and that I hoped they liked vodka tonics. Here is John's brilliant spin on a tailgaters punch that's made in a thermos and makes a mockery of the expected Bloody Mary or can of suds.

TAILGATERS BOURBON BUCK

What You'll Need:

8 ounces bourbon

4 ounces freshly squeezed lemon juice

3 ounces simple syrup

ginger beer

How to Make It: In a thermos or sealable container combine all ingredients except ginger beer. This can be done up to 24 hours ahead of time, but keep it refrigerated. When ready to serve, add 2 cups of ice to the thermos or sealable container. Seal and shake vigorously. Pour liquid into cups over fresh ice and top with 2 ounces of ginger beer. Briefly stir and garnish with a lemon wedge. Or not.

SUMMER: WATERMELON BLAST

I learned this watermelon-ade recipe from an Emeril Lagasse recipe book and tweaked it into a boozy, refreshing summer cocktail. It kills every time. You can prep the "ade" hours ahead or the night before.

WATERMELON BLAST

What You'll Need:

8 cups cubed watermelon (about 1 quart of juice)

1 cup freshly squeezed lime juice

good quality vodka

sparkling wine (Italy's Rotari is a great choice)

1/2 cup sugar

mint leaves

lime wedges for garnish

How to Make It:

For the watermelon-ade: In a blender, whiz the watermelon in batches until smooth and strain over a large bowl; discard the solids. Add lime and sugar to the watermelon juice and stir until the sugar has dissolved. Taste and add more sugar if necessary. Refrigerate until chilled.

For the punch: Combine the watermelon-ade, vodka, and sparkling wine in a punchbowl with a cup of mint leaves. Stir and serve over ice in a highball glass.

AUTUMN: GARDEN CITY SANGRIA

The beauty of this big batch of spiced sangria by Brian Russell, colleague and head bartender at David Burke's King Bar in Garden City, NY, is that it is made with light-bodied Pinot Noir, lending just the right earthiness to balance the rich, spiced reduction. Perfect for spicy food, as well as for pairing with grilled meats such as steak, sausage, and burgers.

GARDEN CITY SANGRIA

What You'll Need:

2 bottles Pinot Noir

14 oz. cognac or apple brandy

28 oz. spiced red wine reduction:

Combine 15–20 cloves, 5 allspice berries, 5 star aniseeds, and 5 cinnamon sticks with 1 bottle of Pinot Noir and 1 cup of sugar. In a medium saucepan, bring to a boil then lower heat to simmer, reducing the liquid by 2/3. Let cool.

How to Make It: Combine ingredients in a large pitcher and refrigerate. Serve over fresh ice in a large stem glass. Garnish with an orange wheel. Fresh diced fruit is optional.

WINTER: OLD FASHIONED COCKTAILS FOR A CROWD

Darren Grenia of Yours Sincerely, Brooklyn, NY, has devoted his entire bar to the concept of large format cocktails, including this big-batch old fashioned recipe that's perfect for a crowd when you don't feel like hanging out behind the bar all night. These measurements fit perfectly in a 750ml liquor bottle for a cool look and easy pouring. Double the recipe for larger gatherings. The recipe is written in milliliters because Grenia finds them more exacting.

OLD FASHIONED COCKTAILS FOR A CROWD

What You'll Need:
1 oz. orange bitters
56 ml. simple syrup
511 ml. bourbon
105 ml. water

How to Make It: Place ingredients in a large bowl or pitcher and stir well. Funnel into an empty liquor or wine bottle, cork it, and store in the fridge. Serve over ice with a pre-cut orange peel garnish.

BONUS! HOW TO MAKE A COSMOPOLITAN

Since a good cosmo is really a drink that needs to be shaken, it doesn't lend well to batching. But it's still a fun party drink, and somebody's always going to want a cosmo. Once you present the pink and delicious modern classic, others will call for one as well. Here is the well-documented original recipe by Toby Cecchini, who came up with the drink in New York City in 1998.

COSMOPOLITAN

What You'll Need:
1.5 oz. lemon vodka
3/4 oz. Cointreau
3/4 oz. lime juice
3/4 oz. cranberry juice

How to Make It: Add ice to the ingredients and shake until chilled. Strain into chilled cocktail glass. Garnish with a lemon twist.

COFFEE IS FOR CLOSERS

Coffee is a way of life for so many humans on this planet that it's become a unifying symbol, something we can all get behind. Whether you are brewing with an Italian moka pot, a Turkish ibrik, or a simple, reliable French press, coffee gets our collective asses out of bed in the morning. And like anything else, if coffee is a part of your life, then it's worth treating yourself to the best. The rich aroma of roasted beans brewed and blended with a little milk and sugar cuts through the fog of a sleepless night, helps keep digestion on an even keel, and tempers the ill effects of being overserved the night before (read: a nasty hangover). There is always time for a cup or two—usually two. And coffee pairs beautifully with a newspaper. Just sayin'.

I certainly do not consider myself a coffee connoisseur. I can't espouse the subtleties of how terroir teases nut flavors from a Sumatran arabica, and when it comes to brewing, a barista I'm not. But I have explored every imaginable type of coffee brewed in myriad styles, and I've learned a few things about the world's second most consumed beverage (water is number one). And it starts with brewing your own.

Commercial coffee brands brewed through drip makers or, gulp, instant cup systems like Keurig are serviceable caffeine vehicles, I concede. But there is no comparison to freshly ground, well-brewed coffee. Instead of settling for a lifetime of average joe, carve out a few extra minutes to trade regular-old for a transcendent experience. All you need is quality beans, a proper vessel, and a few techniques.

FRENCH PRESS

French press coffee produces a distinct and luscious cup that brings out the full expression of a bean with a rich froth. This simple system of steeping and pressing ground beans produces a rich, smooth, and indulgent cup with no paper filter to strain out flavor-packed oils. All this in five minutes, and a quality French press is readily available for about $15–$40.

To use a French press, boil water in a kettle and rinse your coffee pot with the hot water to warm it. Allow the temperature to drop below a boil. Place about three tablespoons of ground beans (French presses work best with a medium coarse grind) for each cup of hot water—eight ounces. Add water, give it a stir, and pop on the cap and plunger (which has a filter that traps the grinds at the bottom of the pot). Let sit for a couple of minutes. Slowly and carefully, push down the plunger. Make sure the lid is in pouring position and serve immediately.

IRISH COFFEE

What You'll Need:

1 1/2 oz. Irish whiskey
1 1/2 oz. strongly brewed coffee (any premium dark roast)
2 tsp. sugar
lightly whipped heavy cream
cinnamon or nutmeg

How to Make It: Add sugar and a touch of hot coffee in glass. Stir to dissolve. Add rest of hot coffee, stir, and add whiskey. To finish, slowly drizzle the lightly whipped (shake the shit out of it for a couple of minutes) cream over the back of a spoon to sit atop the coffee.

COLD BREW

Making killer cold brew is a simple proposition, but it does require you to plan ahead. Learning this "make it once, use it many" technique will cue you up for a work-week's worth of amazing iced coffee that buries anything coming out of an auto drip. Make a large batch of concentrated brew Sunday night for quick, quality coffee all week, or prep up a batch the night before hosting brunch with friends.

To make it, stir together about 5–6 tablespoons of medium ground coffee for every 1.5 cups cold water in a jar. Cover and let rest in the refrigerator overnight up to 18 hours. Double strain through a coffee filter or cheesecloth into a clean jar. It will keep about a week.

To make an iced coffee, fill a tall glass with ice, mix equal parts coffee concentrate with water. Despite the strength of the concentrate, the cold steep process removes much of the coffee's bitterness and makes a smooth, café-quality iced coffee. Or you can make this martini.

KICK-ASS COLD BREW MARTINI

What You'll Need:
2 oz. vodka
3/4 oz. cold brew coffee
3/4 oz. cream
1/2 oz. simple syrup or cane sugar
to taste

How to Make It: Combine ingredients in a shaker and fill halfway with ice. Shake until cold. Strain into a martini glass. Fancy chocolate syrup swirls are optional, but garnish with 3 coffee beans.

PERCOLATOR

After breaking my second glass French press a few years ago, my mother-in-law gave us her antique stovetop percolator and we never looked back. Almost never. I love French press coffee. But this is also a delightful way to begin your day.

A percolator is a pretty low-tech, unassuming piece of equipment; there's no programming, settings, or dials. But under the hood there is a lot going on. The percolator steams coffee in a vacuum setting before the boiling liquid builds up in the tube and filters through the ground beans. I like to cook it on medium high heat. When the coffee's aroma hits my nostrils, I know to take it off the stove in 10 minutes. My wife insists I wait too long. I do not, but if you leave it too long or let it burn, the coffee will taste bitter and metallic.

ESPRESSO

Espresso is strong, black, concentrated coffee that is brewed by forcing steam through finely ground beans. Your local café likely has a fancy espresso machine, and there are many home versions available. But to make a thick, deeply concentrated coffee with a frothy "crema" top, an Italian espresso moka pot is your path to least resistance. Once you have the espresso down, you are on your way to creating java masterpieces like these:

· **Caffè latte:** 3 oz. of steamed milk to a shot (1 oz.) of espresso with a foamy head.

· **Cappuccino:** Here, the steamed milk is in equal proportion to the espresso, which is commonly a double shot, where the steamed milk sits atop the coffee.

· **Macchiato:** Starbucks may have bastardized this concoction of steamed milk and espresso with caramel, but the real deal is simply a layer of espresso and a top layer of milk foam.

· **"Caffè" mocha:** Also called mochachino, what you have here is basically a caffè latte with the addition of cocoa powder, resulting in a sophisticated, highly caffeinated version of a hot chocolate.

· **Americano:** 1 shot of espresso is mixed with about 6 oz. of hot water, and it tastes like a cup of strongly brewed coffee.

COFFEE BEANS

Coffee beans are the seed of a berry found in two species of evergreen shrub: *Coffea arabica* and *Coffea canephora*. These shrubs grow two of the most important commercial beans: arabica and robusta. *Coffea arabica* beans are believed to have originated in the Ethiopian highlands and grow in lower yields at higher altitudes than the *Coffea canephora* beans, making them rarer and more difficult to harvest, which, as a result, makes arabica more expensive. Arabica beans are the superior bean in terms of flavor, aroma, body, and complexity. Robusta beans, which are higher in acidity and caffeine but have harsher flavors, are reserved for canned supermarket brands. Coffee beans flourish between the Tropics of Capricorn and Cancer, and the finest arabica beans are found in East Africa (Sumatra, Ethiopia, Rwanda), Asia Pacific, and Latin and South America (Costa Rica, Nicaragua, Colombia).

Arabica

Robusta

ROASTING BEANS

It's during the roasting process that the coffee develops its flavor character and depth of color. Roasting involves "toasting" the beans in an oven to the desired level of darkness, with your basic range of light, medium, or dark—blends often being a combination of all three. Lightly roasted beans procure a sharp hit of acidity met with light body, a faint aroma, and minimal bitterness. A medium roast brings the fuller expression of the bean into focus with a richer body, balanced acidity, and a bigger aroma. Dark roasted coffees are typically low in acid and high in bitterness. Often, low-quality beans are dark roasted to mask quality defects, especially in mass market brands.

PART TWO: FOOD

HOW TO COOK A STEAK

Cooking a steak is not a recipe. It's a technique. And once this simple skill is perfected, it can be easily applied to almost any protein for a lifetime of quick, healthy, delicious meals. The ability to cook a beautifully seared, caramelized tender sirloin is worth the investment in time it takes to master it a million times over. To get you there, I asked veteran chef and friend Michael Lippi to explain how to make a classic steak (based on a 1.5"–1.75" steak) frites at home. Here is what he said.

STEP ONE: POTATOES

You want to put your oven on 425 degrees, and while it's warming up, slice a Russett potato lengthwise into quarters so they look like big French fries. Drizzle some olive oil and hit it with some seasoning. I season everything. Pop it the oven once it's at temperature, and set the timer for about 40 minutes.

STEP TWO: STEAK

What I should've said first was take your steak out of the fridge. The temperature of the meat will affect your cooking time, which is why you may have followed recipes to find your steak came out raw. Anyway, let's say the steak is room temperature. Season it on both sides. You are ideally going to want to use a cast iron pan. Thin metal pieces of shit don't hold temperature, and if you have a pan with a plastic handle on it, it can't go into the oven. Get your pan on the stove, and put some medium high heat on it with a little oil, just enough to coat the pan. When the oil gets hot, you are going to see it just begin to kick up smoke. Not burn, mind you, pay attention. But once it's at that smoke point, lay your steak down. It should sizzle. Keep it there for a good five minutes. This will put on a nice sear. It's that caramelization that gives you lots of flavor. Flip it over, and sear up the other side, then it's time to finish it in the oven with your potatoes.

When you pop your steak in there, feel free to throw in some crushed garlic cloves if you like. Now, one thing I recommend is to get a cooking thermometer. They cost about $8 and are your secret weapon to a perfect steak every time. Numbers don't lie. In about 10 minutes, stick your thermometer into the center of the meat. Medium rare is about 130 degrees, medium 145, and medium-well is 160 degrees. But here's the best part. Just before it's done, throw in a couple of tablespoons of butter. When it melts, baste the meat with it. Now you're talkin'.

STEP THREE: SALAD

The salad? Just throw a handful of arugula in a bowl and hit it with some olive oil, lemon juice, salt, and pepper. The bitter greens and citrus will brighten up your steak and potatoes. Enjoy with a nice glass of Cabernet. You're done.

BRING THE HEAT

Playing with fire was a game back in the day, and a plate of chicken wings was the hot sauce gameboard on which we played. A few buddies and I would sidle up to the bar and challenge the chef to make the hottest damn wings they could muster. They obliged, unleashing assaults so furious my mouth still tingles. As those wings arrived, cold draft beers were placed before us. We ate. We sweated. We suffered. The first one to touch the beer paid for the round and finished the plate. Nobody touched the beer. It was awesome.

What I didn't realize then is why I was enjoying the pain so much. I had no idea that the reason sweat poured off my head, my eyes watered up, and my nose began to run was that it was the capsaicin in the habanero sauce that was causing my brain to dispatch vast amounts of endorphins, which block pain, and dopamine, the stuff that lets you feel pleasure, into my system, a natural rush called a pepper buzz.

The craft pepper scene is a tale of two hot sauces. Supermarkets are flooded with alleged "craft" sauces with slick packaging and often psychotic heat claims that are hardly craft at all. Then there's the real deal: sauces made with fresh, U.S.-grown, world-class pasteurized peppers. Essentially hot sauce is pasteurized peppers and vinegar. Sauce makers build flavors on top of this base or choose to keep it simple. Here's the difference:

"Craft" hot sauces are easy to spot, usually by heavy salt content. Sauce makers purchase bulk peppers, grown overseas and placed in huge vats with water and salt. The concoction ferments on a ship on the way over. What arrives in port, at this point, is inedible, basically poison. These inexpensive pepper concentrates are transferred to 55-gallon drums that then ship to co-packers around the country, who sell the same commodity to companies both large and small. However, none of them are artisanal craft sauces.

Here's the thing. These sauces do tend to be hot. Typical craft sauces are often at least twenty-five times hotter than your average bottle of Tabasco Sauce and go up from there, so the upper echelon of craft is not recommended for the uninitiated. The record holder for the world's hottest pepper, the Pepper X, is Eddie Currie, who happens to be my cousin. He, along with fellow pepper-heads, preaches that high levels of capsaicin, a phenolic amide that gives peppers their heat, is a miracle food that has a host of benefits, like boosting metabolism and heart rate to create lots of energy. According to Currie, capsaicin also affects increases in white blood cells, which protect your body from disease.

Levels of capsaicin in pepper are measured in Scoville Heat Units (SHU). Heat units in peppers range in scale from zero to infinity, and currently they top out with the Carolina Reaper at around 2.3 million and Pepper X at 3 million, both grown by Smokin' Ed Currie. Here is how some common peppers land on the SHU scale:

SCOVILLE HEAT UNITS (SHU)

PEPPERS:

Bell Pepper:	0
Jalapeno and Chipotle:	2,5000–8,000
Serrano:	10,000–23,000
Cayenne:	30,000–50,000
Habanero and Scotch Bonnet:	100,000–350,000
Ghost Pepper:	1,465,000
Carolina Reaper:	2,300,000
Pepper X:	3,000,000

COMMERCIAL PEPPER SAUCE:

Frank's Red Hot:	450
Huy Fong Sriracha (Rooster Sauce):	2,200
Tabasco:	2,500
Crystal:	3,000
El Yucateco:	5,000

SEVEN AWESOME CRAFT HOT SAUCES

When it comes to the hot stuff, the ingredients are what separate the men from the boys. The best sauces get their heat from fresh peppers, while imposters rely on extract, which is basically chemicals, with no pepper at all—a red flag indicating a lesser-quality sauce. Companies rely on extract to boost heat levels instead of paying for a natural pepper. Chemicals are cheap.

Peppers are expensive. Here is some of the best stuff on the market right now. But don't be fooled by the mild-hot scale. It's all spicy.

① SECRET AARDVARK (PORTLAND, OR)

Heat Scale: 1/10 (Somewhere in the realm of Tabasco Sauce)

If a condiment could be a hipster, this would be it. Secret Aardvark Trading Company was founded in Portland, Oregon, in 2004 and has built a cult following that began in farmers' markets and whose line has grown to become Amazon's third best-selling hot sauce. The flagship is habanero-based, described by the company as "Caribbean meets Tex-Mex." Fans cite Aardvark's curious ability to adapt to the food it pairs with as the object of their obsession. This is the mildest sauce on the list by a landslide.

② TRUFF HOT SAUCE (LOS ANGELES, CA)

Heat Scale: 3/10

Truff combines fresh chili peppers, pricy Italian black truffle oil, and agave nectar from Jalisco, Mexico (Hello, tequila pairing!), to create this earthy, funky, hot-but-not-too-hot sauce. Truffle oil fans enjoy this sauce as a brilliant topping and killer secret weapon in the kitchen, rocking it in anything from meat rubs to grilled cheeses.

③ HUMBOLDT EMERALD SAUCE (HUMBOLDT, CA)

Heat Scale: 4/10

This "mild" sauce is only mellow by the hottest standards, so it's not for beginners. Humboldt was started in California by Daniel Bixler and Chef Cal Ferris, two friends who focus on fresh, high-pepper-content sauces with low sodium, and the company has grown to become a household name among connoisseurs. Emerald is the mildest in Humbolt's line, with a habanero base, accompanied by roasted peppers, lime, cilantro, and ginger, giving this green sauce a bright citrusy taste that wakes up Asian, Mexican, and Caribbean dishes in a big, spicy way.

④ BRAVADO SPICE BOYS GHOST PEPPER & BLUEBERRY (HOUSTON, TX)

Heat Scale: 5/10

While the idea of combining heavy spice and viscous blueberry might sound like an awesome idea, if you're the type that needs a glass of milk after a dot of Cholula, the ghost pepper heat source in this Bravado's Spice Boys offering probably isn't for you. But in terms of what the ghost can deliver, it's a palatable way to feel the heat and explore the pepper's deep, rich flavors at the same time.

⑤ KARMA SAUCE EXTREME (PITTSFORD, NY)

Heat Scale: 6/10

It's one thing to savor the unique balance of Karma's apple, honey, and butternut squash flavors, but you'll likely be more focused on the up to 1 million SHU of brutal heat delivered by a blistering blend of peppers including Trinidad Moruga scorpions and ghosts. Fans contend that while Extreme Karma is, by any definition, f***ing hot, they insist the sauce retains its earthy winter vegetable flavor. All I taste is pain.

⑥ BIG FATS OCTO MAXIMUS (CHICAGO, IL)

Heat Scale: 8/10

Big Fats Octo Maximus bills itself as a northern Indian spice blend. The star of this show is the "seven pot primo," a cross between the scorching Naga Morich and the viscous 7 Pot pepper. While this sauce allegedly works magic on grilled vegetables, potatoes, chicken wings, shrimp tacos, chili, and of course, Indian dishes, I couldn't tell you since I tapped out with the Karma.

⑦ PUCKERBUTT REAPER SQUEEZINS (FORT MILL, SC)

Heat Scale: On a scale of 1–10, this is an 11

Puckerbutt is the mac daddy of all pepper sauces, the pinnacle of growers and purveyors against which all others are measured, and it is also the only hot sauce that's certified USDA organic. The fiery pepper cult leader is Smokin' Ed Currie, world record holder for growing the hottest peppers known to man: the Carolina Reaper and Pepper X. Puckerbutt's biggest, hottest, freshest hot sauce of them all is Reaper Squeezins—a harmless sounding little sauce that contains 94% reaper pepper—about 1.8 million Scoville units that will blow your head right off your body if disrespected. Carolina Reapers have a burn that strikes hard and immediate and is backed up with a second wave of heat that builds over time. Google "reaper pepper challenge" to see what can happen. It's OK to fear the reaper. I do.

THE JOY OF CHEESE

You know that cheese is something special when it ranks as the number one stolen food. *Time* magazine reported that 4% of all cheese in the world is shoplifted, and frankly, it makes sense. It's not only pocket-sized, but it's also one of the most nutritious and delectable foods known to man.

There are plenty of important reasons to steal cheese, especially these days as we are amid a massive renaissance. Back in the day, European immigrants from cheese culture countries like Switzerland, France, Italy, Germany, and the Netherlands brought Old World traditions from their home countries to the United States, and the local artisanal cheese scene flourished. Eventually, industrial methods and large-scale farming took root, all but wiping out the local scene. It was in the '70s when baby boomers began to demand organic and whole foods, and artisanal cheesemaking rebounded. Today, cheesemaking has been elevated in the United States to an art form on par with European cheese. Simply put, the quality of modern cheese blows away what was available thirty years ago.

Making quality cheese begins with the animal. Top-notch husbandry, milk production, and craftsmanship all contribute to the production of an exceptional cheese. The most excellent cheese comes from well-raised animals that have access to a diversity of plant species, quality water, and proper care. For the best stuff, seek out raw-milk cheese, as opposed to cheese made with pasteurized milk. During pasteurization, the milk is heated up to high temperatures, killing colonies of microbes and bacteria that produce the healthiest and most exciting cheeses. Not that pasteurized milk cheese is bad, but raw-milk cheese is the real deal. Another mark of quality is artisanal cheese made with minimal machinery. The best way to purchase cheese, especially soft cheese, is from its source, in farm country, where local cheesemakers often sell their products at wholesale prices. They're found in rural areas as well as in the mountains, like in Colorado, the Pacific Northwest, and Vermont, where some of the best stuff in the States is being made right now. Farmers' markets, where the cheesemakers come to you, can also be a an excellent source.

Cheese is made everywhere in so many styles that the idea of wrapping your head around it all could drive you into a fetal position. Complicated as cheese may be, remember this: it's worth understanding. The finest cheeses are sublime. And don't be intimidated: cheese is just fermented milk that's preserved by reducing its water content. It's not complicated, but it is vast. Exploring some iconic old-school cheeses is your ticket to navigating a cheese plate, so let's delve into the realm of what enthusiasts call the world's most perfect food. Nourishing, perfectly textured, and ethereal.

SEVEN HUNKS OF CHEESE GUARANTEED TO IMPROVE YOUR LIFE

UNITED STATES QUESO DE MANO

Type: Goat milk
Perfect Wine Pairing: Chardonnay, Pinot Noir, Merlot
People tend to either love or hate goat cheese, but those who hate it have probably never tried Queso de Mano from the Haystack Dairy in Colorado. This simple pressed raw-milk cheese was inspired by a Spanish cheese of the same name and has come to find a

place in the upper echelon of American cheesemaking. Milky, creamy, grassy, and herbaceous, this perennial award winner spreads across the tongue and finishes with a sweet, fresh, goat-milk flavor, not a dirty barnyard. And it doesn't hurt that Haystack is distributed nationally, so it's not impossible to find.

SPANISH MANCHEGO

Type: Sheep milk
Perfect Wine Pairing: Sherry
It's hard to go wrong with Manchego. The quintessential cheese of Spain, a mellow, rich crowd pleaser, is always a welcome addition to a cheese plate. Real Manchego is a denomination de origen and easy to identify by its zigzag markings on the side of the rind. Once inside, Manchego is ivory in color. Somehow the cheese manages to be firm and dry, yet creamy and rich at the same time. It's not likely you will come across raw-milk Manchego due to EU regulations, but that aside it's a traditionally made cheese. As the Manchego ages, it picks up nutty, caramel flavors and ends with a briny finish. Manchego is at its peak aged between 6 months to a year.

ENGLISH CHEDDAR

Type: Cow milk
Perfect Wine Pairing: Grenache, Merlot, Pinot Noir
Cheddar is a somewhat modern style tracing back to the 16th century near England's Cheddar Gorge in the Mendip Hills, where it was made in caves perfect for aging. Since then, cheddar has become a standard style throughout the world. Its appeal lies in its sustainability as well as its adaptability. Cheddar tends to pair well

with almost anything you throw its way, especially beer. California, Vermont, Wisconsin, and the western coast of Scotland are all sources of fine cheddar, but what's considered the finest is farmhouse cheddar from southwest England, the cheese that has been called "England's gift to humanity." For me, it's simply the best representation of a familiar flavor that's part of our DNA.

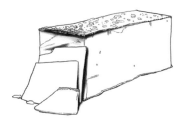

SWISS GRUYÈRE

Type: Cow milk
Perfect Wine Pairing: Burgundy Red (or cognac)

In Europe, the great cheese regions arc in an oval on the map, stretching from the top of Spain into southwest France, through south-central France, over to Germany and western Austria, and then settling down into the top half of Italy. And right in the heart of that arc is Switzerland, whose cheeses are famous throughout the world. The most famous Swiss cheese of them all is Gruyère, a terroir-driven, raw-milk masterpiece with nutty, earthy flavors coupled with sweetness, gaining extraordinary complexity as it ages, which is generally between 4 to 12 months.

ITALIAN PARMIGIANO REGGIANO (PARMESAN)

Type: Cow milk
Perfect Wine Pairing: Primitivo or Zinfindel

The best of the white stuff that sits atop your bowl of spaghetti is considered one of the great cheeses on the planet: the mighty Parmigiano Reggiano. The real Parmesan is made exclusively in a handful of Italian provinces, including Modena, Parma, and Reggio Emilia. The real deal is going to be moister and sweeter than its many imitators. The skim milk used to make the cheese comes from cows that are required to be grass, hay, or alfalfa fed only, and experts can detect how the flavors change with the animal's diet from season to season. Parmesan ages 18 to 36 months and is best enjoyed in large chunks but obviously grates well on top of soup, sauce, and salad. Its flakiness melts in the mouth, devolving into a complex world of fragrant and savory flavors.

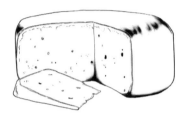

DUTCH GOUDA

Type: Cow milk
Perfect Wine Pairing: Cabernet Sauvignon

The Netherlands established naval trade routes that opened the door to our modern-day global economy, and Gouda, Holland's cheese, has been traded throughout Europe and beyond since the 12th century. Today, the Netherlands produces about 730,000 metric tons of cheese, and its beloved Gouda, pronounced "Howda," accounts for 60% of the world's cheese consumption. Young Gouda is fruity, supple, and sweet, and it kicks ass as a snack or the main event on a sandwich. As it ages, Gouda evolves into a grainy, salty, tangy, sharp cheese that's almost crunchy. The best of the best is farmhouse Gouda, called Boerenkaas, a raw-milk cheese made by small farmers with dairy from grass-fed cows.

FRENCH BLUE CHEESE

Type: Cow, sheep, goat milk
Perfect Wine Pairing: Port, Sauternes

Cheese experts estimate that France has around 1,000 varieties of cheese, and the most celebrated of them all is most certainly the French bleu,

Roquefort. Blue is a mold-ripened cheese. Blue molds are part of the penicillin family and occur naturally or are added by the cheesemaker. The "bleu" is the flower of the mold, which ripens the cheese in part by breaking down the fats and proteins, making the cheese, in a sense, pre-digested. Sweet Italian Gorgonzola, mild Bavarian "blu" from Germany, and rich British Stilton (which is said to cause odd, vivid dreams) are all blues, but the best in class is Roquefort, a sheep milk bleu considered one of France's national treasures, known for its rich but mild creaminess. Anybody can check it out. Roquefort is relatively easy to find.

WHY PAIRING WINE AND CHEESE IS EASY

While it's true enough that specific wines pair sublimely with certain cheeses, there's no need to obsess. Chances are, the cheese in your fridge and the wine in your rack will taste fine together. Just ask the French, who tend to pop the wine they like to drink and eat the cheese they think tastes best, and just go for it. No one's overthinking the pairing. They are simply eating lunch.

THE ART OF CHARCUTERIE

Before hunting in the meat aisle at their local Piggly Wiggly, humans figured out that meat could be preserved by smoking it or curing it with salt. What started out as a necessity for survival evolved over time into one of our greatest culinary arts: charcuterie. Thousands of years later, seasoning, fermenting, and other techniques have elevated the craft to producing the bacon, sausages, hams, and pâtés on which we indulge in all corners of civilization.

Charcuterie (shär-,kü-tə-'rē), whose Latin translation is "flesh" (char) and "cooked" (cuit), traces its lineage back to the 15th century in France. The term was initially assigned to charcutiers, purveyors of pork and offal products, the hipster butchers of the day, and their charcuterie was not unlike what you find in your local deli. Today, the term "charcuterie" is synonymous with the art of curing meats. What began as a peasant dish of animal fat and salt blossomed into a global culinary movement.

While Spain is best known for its salt-cured jamón serrano, and Italy contributes the world's most beloved sausages and salamis, the United States' greatest charcuterie contribution is the hot dog. Hot dogs first appeared in the carts of street vendors in New York City around 1860, and the first stand opened in Coney Island in Brooklyn in about 1870, hawking an estimated 4,000 in its first year. Today, we eat billions of these easy to handle, inexpensive meals on a bun.

Whether making hot dogs, curing ham, or crafting the most excellent salami, the unifying factor here is curing with salt. Curing is a preservation and flavoring technique in which salt is added to meats or vegetables to leach out water content through the process of osmosis. From there, different cuts of pork with different coarseness and fat content are minced to create specific textures, flavors, and hardness, which is typically determined by the duration of aging. Ultimately, the quality of cured meat comes down to ingredients and the skill of the craftsman producing it. Here is a glance at some of the most celebrated charcuterie in which to indulge.

A CHARCUTERIE PLATE

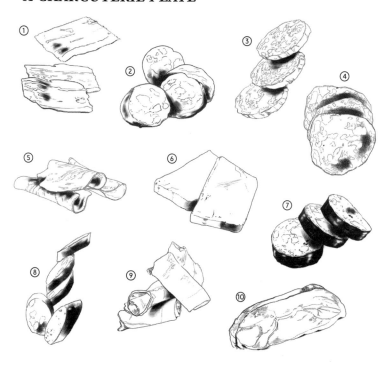

① JAMÓN SERRANO, SPAIN

Beautiful in its simplicity, this ham is the cured leg of a pig, packed in salt, hung to dry for up to four years, then sliced thin, imparting intense flavors and a melt-in-your-mouth texture. The pinnacle of Spanish ham is jamón Ibérico, made from a breed of free-range black-footed pigs from the Iberian Peninsula that are raised on a diet of acorns and which is considered among the finest cuts of meat on the planet.

② CHORIZO, SPAIN

Pork loin, jowl, belly (pancetta), shoulder, and back fat are combined with herbs, garlic, and a ton of real Spanish paprika known as pimentón to comprise the main stuffins' in Spanish chorizo. This cured, dried, spicy sausage, Spain's version of Italian salami, is stuffed into hog or beef casing and served as tapas on Spanish menus. Chorizo's flavor runs between spicy, sweet, and smoky, depending on the maker's recipe. Don't confuse Spanish chorizo with the raw Mexican variety. While both are delicious, they're not interchangeable.

③ SALAMI, ITALY

Salami has been made for at least 2,000 years, and the term describes pretty much any Italian sausage derived from ground, seasoned meat stuffed into a casing and dried. The duration of drying dictates the hardness of the salami. Predictively, different regions in Italy produce different styles. Genoa salami is made with pork, salt, garlic, pepper, fennel, and wine, while finocchiona from Tuscany is a spicier version, flavored with fennel seeds and black pepper. Sweet Milano salami is made from a pork and beef combination and incorporates flecks of pork fat. Salami cotto is a cooked sausage from Italy's Piedmont region that is seasoned with garlic and peppercorns.

④ SOPPRESSA AND SOPPRESSATA, ITALY

Soppressa and soppressata are dry-cured pork sausages, similar to salami, whose meat is smoked, pressed into a casing, and hung to dry. Soppressa is produced in the northeast, Veneto, and Frioul, the most famous being soppressa Vicentina. Soppressata comes from the southern regions of Basilicata, Apulia, and Calabria, where they produce funky, oblong, hand-packed sausages. Soppressata di Calabria's signature ingredient is hot pepper, and soppressata di Puglia's hallmark is a chunk of lard, serving as the fat source, which has been combined with leaner pieces of meat.

⑤ PROSCIUTTO, ITALY

Most European cuisines have their own version of prosciutto, which is seasoned, cured, air-dried ham. It's Italy's answer to Spain's jamón serrano. Like most Italian food, the flavor and quality of your prosciutto is dictated by where it's made, since any cured meat ultimately gets its flavor from where the animal is raised. The most celebrated is prosciutto di Parma, whose salty, sweet, and nutty flavor derives from the local pigs' diet of parmesan cheese whey. San Daniele prosciutto is another iconic delicacy whose lean, sweet meat comes from Italian pigs, sea salt, and fresh air.

⑥ PÂTÉ, FRANCE

French charcuterie is unique in its use of terrines or torchons, which are molds used to form the charcuterie shape, instead of casings. Pâté is a spreadable paste made from a mixture of meat and fat from calves' livers, pheasant, and wild boar, with a wide range of herbs, coriander, mushrooms, brandy, and wine. The richest, most buttery and decadent pâté of them all is the ethically challenged foi gras made from the engorged liver of a force-fed duck or goose. Quality French foi can be difficult to find in the States, so well-made domestic options make excellent substitutes.

⑦ BLOOD PUDDING, IRELAND

While blood pudding is made all over the world, nobody does it quite like the Irish, whose legendary breakfast of fried eggs, potatoes, Irish bacon, grilled tomato, and baked beans isn't complete without black pudding, made with grains, spices, and blood and served in pubs throughout the old country. The most sought-after Irish blood pudding is called drisheen, which is known for its mix of animal blood and its gelatinous texture.

⑧ CHINESE SAUSAGE, CHINA

Honestly, there are too many Chinese sausages from different provinces to even scratch the surface of Chinese cured meats, but one sausage worth noting that's available in Chinese markets in the United States is lap cheong. This sweet, smoky, thick, red, and chewy pork sausage has a high fat content and is flavored with Eastern flavors like rose water, soy, saki, rice vinegar, and sugar.

⑨ SPECK, GERMANY, ITALY, AUSTRIA, AND SPAIN

Speck is a juniper-flavored ham in English-speaking culinary circles. In Italy, "speck" refers to a strain of smoked prosciutto. German speck is identical to the Italian "lardo," which is a type of salumi, or appetizer, made by curing the thick layer of fatback with herbs and spices. Gailtaler speck from Austria is one of the finest hams in the world and has been produced by expert charcutiers for over 600 years.

⑩ JAMBON DE BAYONNE, FRANCE

France's answer to Italian prosciutto or Spanish jamón Ibérico is jambon de Bayonne, a dry-cured ham that has been produced in the southwest of France for about 1,000 years. Like its Spanish cousin, Bayonne ham is made from a simple combination of locally raised pork from the area around the Adour Basin and salt that is sourced by evaporating salt water from the Reine Jeanne D'Oraas spring; it is then aged in a region where humidity coming off the Atlantic collides with drier air from the Pyrenees, creating magical drying conditions.

THE WORLD IS YOUR OYSTER

Adventurous eaters have been feasting on oysters for 2,000 years, and if you count yourself among them, you understand the pleasure these bright, briny, creamy, sweet, herbaceous, mineral, and fruity bivalves contribute to humanity. It's all about hitting great restaurants or seaside clam shacks to indulge in the freshest shellfish you can find, ideally washing them down with a cheap, cold beer or crisp Champagne. If you're not hip to the decadent world of oysters, it's time to get excited about these salty, slippery, slightly dangerous shelled morsels.

It's a great time to eat oysters. Vibrant, healthy beds are producing primo seafood right now, and raising oysters is a growing small-producer industry that provides tons of fresh, sustainable seafood. Eastern oysters stretch along the shallow coastal waters from Newfoundland, past New England, around Florida, into the Gulf of Mexico, and all the way to Argentina. Pacific Oysters cover the west coast of North America, stretching from Alaska straight south to the Baja Peninsula of Mexico. On the East Coast, the most coveted oysters come from the northern stretch of coastline from Newfoundland down through New England, Long Island, and New Jersey. West Coast oysters are mostly coming out of Hood Canal and the Puget Sound, as well as Northern California and British Columbia.

When it comes to finding the best oysters, rule #1 is to buy as locally as possible. The closest stuff is likely to be the freshest since it takes less time to travel to market, and it also helps to support the economy of whatever region you are in. The next thing is to understand that seasons matter. An oyster will taste its best when the water is the coldest. A Long Island Blue Point will eat better in January than it will in August, so in the summer on either coast, order oysters from the coldest water. When it comes to oysters on the half shell, the most in-demand raw oysters tend to come from colder waters. Warmer climate varieties like Virginia's Chesapeake grow in warm, muddy water, are less expensive than cold-water Canadian oysters, and are best suited for frying, making sauces, or a plate of Oyster Rockefeller.

Producers love naming their oysters, creating endless names and types. Keep things simple by separating oysters between East and West Coast varieties. From there, note the farms and regions in which the oysters grow, and you will develop a knowledge of the major producers in your area. While it can be tough to tell East Coast and West Coast oysters apart, there is a distinct difference in taste between the two. As a rule, Pacific oysters are sweeter and brinier and the meat is thicker than that of their East Coast cousins, which are going to be less briny, mineral-forward, and a bit easier to swallow.

Once you separate East and West Coast oysters, the sheer volume of brand names can make choosing an oyster confusing, which is why it's a good idea to order by seasonality and proximity and to take note of the farms the oysters you sample come from. They will become familiar over time. Oysters typically arrive on ice with lemon slices, cocktail sauce, and a mignonette sauce of red-wine vinegar and shallots. There should also be hot sauce on the table. Ask your server which ones are freshest and dive in.

A DOZEN OYSTERS

EAST COAST

BEAU SOLEIL

New Brunswick, Canada

Availability: Mostly year-round. Short lapses occur seasonally.

Pronounced "Boo-show-lay," these small, briny, deep-cupped beauties are crowd pleasers that are considered "starter" oysters in professional circles, but I never get tired of them. Beau Soleils are farmed in Miramichi Bay, New Brunswick, topping out at only about 2.5 inches long after four years of maturity. Beau Soleil is a beautiful expression of an East Coast oyster with a classically clean, fleshy, briny, and yeasty flavor that is a natural pairing with a glass of dry Champagne.

WELLFLEET

Cape Cod, Massachusetts

Availability: September–July

Wellfleets are hugely famous oysters that have been harvested for hundreds of years outside of Cape Cod. Cold, clean water, fast tides, and high salinity come together to produce some of the most popular East Coast oysters, with a signature light body; salty and sweet balanced flavor; and slick, clean, and briny finish. I reach for the lemon and hot sauce when I eat these.

MALPEQUE

Prince Edward Island, Canada

Availability: May–November

Malpeques are what put PEI oysters on the map when they were judged Best Oyster at a Paris exhibition in 1900, making this region world famous. Today these wild oysters are about as household name as an oyster can be. You'll find that they are commonly available at raw bars. At 3.25 inches long, Malpeques are straight down-the-road oysters with moderate brine, a sharp bite, and a short, clean finish. They're a perfect choice for a tableful of friends.

BLUE POINT
Great South Bay, Long Island
Availability: September–July
By New York law, true blue points must be raised in Long Island's Great South Bay for a minimum of three months to qualify, but the term "blue point" remains one of the most "stolen" oyster types and has become almost synonymous with any Atlantic oyster, such as Connecticut or Virginia blue points. But real Long Islanders can tell the difference between the blue points from the Sound and real deal out of the Great South Bay, 4-inch oysters with a crisp texture, mellow flavor, and a briny finish.

ISLAND CREEK
Duxbury Bay, Massachusetts
Availability: Year-round
Shallow, salty, and frigid waters and a twice-a-day tidal exchange are what makes Duxbury Bay such unique and special oyster-producing waters. While there are at least 15 million oysters living in Duxbury Bay, Island Creeks are considered among the finest. Classic butter-and-brine is the hallmark of this salty oyster, which makes it a natural pairing with a crisp sparkling wine or even a cold beer.

BELON
Damariscotta River, Maine
Availability: September–November
A real belon is grown in France's Brittany region, but this Maine-bred European flat is as close as you will get to the real thing in these here parts, and there's a similar version produced on the West Coast. As the name suggests, a belon is a flat-shelled oyster that is primarily raised in Maine. They don't have big

cups on them like blue points or a Malpeques, but they are still large, and their allure lies in their signature mineral flavor and firm bite.

WEST COAST

KUMAMOTO

Oakland Bay, Washington

Availability: Year-round

Small, sweet, creamy, fruity, and a slight brininess come together to yield what is routinely referred to as the "ultimate oyster"—as in everybody loves them. "Kumies" are originally from Japan but are now cultivated in Washington's Chapman Cove, Oakland Bay, and Puget Sound. You can spot a Kumo by its green, deep pocket, grooved ridge shell. Kumamotos are also awesome because they spawn later than other oysters and therefore peak well into summertime, making them a great warm weather choice. Some of the best are from Taylor Shellfish Farms.

SWEETWATER PACIFICS

Tomales Bay, California

Availability: September–July

Pacific oysters are among the most widely cultivated oyster, and one of the best in class is the Sweetwater oyster from Hog Island Oyster Company in Northern California's Tomales Bay. Not only do Pacific oysters deliver a beautiful balance of salty and sweet, Hog Island's oysters are held in a tank and purified after harvest, wisely giving diners an extra layer of purity.

LITTLE SKOOKUM

Puget Sound, Washington

Availability: September–May

These stealthy little bag-to-beach-raised oysters are named after the inlet in the Puget Sound from which they spawn, which is basically a giant soup bowl full of shellfish. Skookums are considered a decent value oyster because up in the Puget Sound it's common to see a Kumamoto bed sitting next to a Skookum bed, and neither is rarer or more challenging to raise than the other. However, Kumamotos usually cost more because they are well-marketed, thus well-known. Little Skookum oysters have soft, fat, and buttery meat with musky, vegetal notes and low brine.

FANNY BAY

Baynes Sound, British Colombia
Availability: Year-round

In the town off the British Canadian coastline of Vancouver Island from which the oyster is both farmed and named, Fanny Bays have been around since the '80s and have been a reliable source of BC oysters around the United States ever since. They are smooth, full-bodied, and steeped in minerality. Reaching about 2.75" at peak, Fanny Bays set the bar for what a BC oyster should be: a solid, consistent product with a reputation for focused quality control that works on the grill or on the half shell.

OLYMPIA

Puget Sound, Washington
Availability: November–March

Back in the day, the famed River Café in Brooklyn served these minuscule but potent Olys (oh-lees) with a dot of caviar, which washed down beautifully with a nice glass of Champagne. Briny, sweet, and metallic, these quarter-sized oysters are primarily from the southern tip of the Puget Sound but are farmed up and down the coast into British Columbia. Experts are convinced that it's the Olys' small stature that makes them less popular than larger Atlantic and Pacific varieties, but while they rarely sell on their own, they sure are popular on a tasting platter.

HUMP ISLAND

Ketchikan, Alaska

Availability: Year-round

Try to get your hands on these hyper-cold-water oysters from a unique region of southeast Alaska where it takes four years for the melon-, mineral-, and brine-flavored oysters to fully mature, as it's about as cold a water in which an oyster can thrive. These are the perfect oysters to seek out in the summertime, while most of the stuff in the lower 48 is spawning. Alaskan oysters are snappy, fleshy, and fresh.

HOW TO SHUCK AN OYSTER

You are best off using a shucker to open oysters, which is readily available for just a couple of bucks. You will also need a towel. And an oyster. If you are right-handed, hold the oyster in the cloth from the front in your left hand (and opposite if you're a lefty). Use the shucker to shimmy into the groove of the oyster in the hinge between the two shells and move it down gently to dig into the groove until you feel it catch. Now twist and pry the oyster open, careful not to create shards of the shell, and remove. Use the same tool to detach the muscle from the shell and move on. It takes a little practice and finesse to master the technique, but once you get the hang of it, you'll whip through them.

PART THREE: CIGARS

HAVE A CIGAR

For most, cigars are a festive indulgence. A stogie is a tradition at the Kentucky Derby, at the birth of a child, or when spending the afternoon on the golf course. Beyond the surface of the occasional celebratory cigar, serious smokers know a world of relaxation and contemplation enveloped in a beautiful, terroir-driven puff of smoke. Learning to enjoy a cigar is an approachable pleasure that starts with a casual smoke and then becomes increasingly complex and more rewarding the deeper you explore. Once you fall in love, it's a hard relationship to break. Be careful.

Cigars are made with three main components: filler, which is the tobacco; a binder leaf, which holds it together and gives it shape; and a wrapper leaf, the best of which have gorgeous color and an impressive roll and will impart at least half of a cigar's flavor. The color of the wrapper also helps one successfully commandeer a cigar purchase, as it almost always dictates how bold, strong, and dark the flavor will be. The darker the wrapper leaf, the heavier the cigar.

When deciding on a cigar, choose the color you like your coffee to be. It's not a perfect method, but it's a decent starting-off point. You experience similar levels of spice and boldness from a cigar that you would from the strain of your morning joe. If you drink double espressos all day, chances are you'll prefer a darker leaf. Milk-and-sugar guys might like something lighter. The darkness of the leaf comes from sun exposure, which increases mineral content and nicotine. Darker leaves taste meatier, while lighter leaves are milder, imparting flavors such as almond and tea.

Like wine or whiskey, there are hierarchies of cigar quality: machine-made, fixed-filler, and premium handmade. Machine-made cigars typically contain "short filler," a paper shredder version of tobacco that goes through factory presses, putting everything in the right place. Fixed-filler cigars have a blend of short filler and longer tobacco leaves and can be either hand-rolled or machine-made. But if short-fill tobacco is merely trimmings, the long-fill tobacco is the primo tobacco. That's what you look for in a cigar. When searching for a cigar for an occasion, these are the cigars you want. They're best purchased at a tobacconist, inside a humidor, though there are many great online options to choose from. Not everybody has a neighborhood tobacconist.

The length of a cigar dictates how long you are going to smoke it. An 8-inch Double Corona (FC) or a 7-inch Churchill size will last at least an hour if you burn it the right way. Something that's 3.5–4 inches can go for 30–40 minutes. A cigar's thickness is called ring gauge and is less a question of flavor than of comfort. People gravitate towards fatter cigars believing they're a better value. Truth is, you are not really tasting all that tobacco, so find something that feels comfortable in your mouth (Settle down, Beavis).

Cigars are susceptible to drying out and should ideally be kept at 70% humidity and at about 70 degrees F (21 degrees C). Kept in optimal conditions, cigars will last 100 years or more. But leaving cigars out for extended periods will cause them to dry unevenly, wreaking havoc on your smoking experience.

CHOOSING THE PERFECT CIGAR

Whether you are a beginner or an aficionado, here's how to pick the right cigar for the right occasion.

IT'S A BABY: CIGARS FOR THE BEGINNER CROWD

When it comes to buying cigars for an uninitiated crowd, look for a Robusto in a light wrapper. Robusto is the perfect pick, or else you are going to see waste because people are going to put them down. While a 64 gauge is an inch, find a 50–52 ring, which seems to be a comfortable size for most people.

Robusto

Davidoff

Arturo Fuente

For a true beginner's smoke, seek out what aficionados call a morning cigar, which uses Connecticut Shade. This is a wrapper that originated in the States but today generally refers to the seed varietal, not the location, and is mainly grown in Ecuador. The leaf is grown in the shade, which forces a light color and mild flavor. A good one will have a nice minerality to it. Davidoff is a luxury brand that uses a lot of Ecuadorian Connecticut Shade. But the real deal comes from the Connecticut River Valley, so check out Holt's cigar company for a range of styles.

A cigar with a Cameroon wrapper is another excellent choice for beginners, and seasoned smokers appreciate it as well. The Fuente Hemingway series has a red chestnut color and tends to be slightly sweet—not in a flavored, artificial way, but it has some red fruit brightness. The Arturo Fuente rolls are reliable starter cigars with mild to medium filler. The presentation is excellent, they are fun to smoke, and they are relatively short. They're a surefire crowd pleaser for a group of guys and gals with various experiences.

A BACHELOR PARTY HERE, A GOLF OUTING THERE: INTERMEDIATE

Take things to the next level by springing for Nicaraguan cigars. You may encounter an Ecuadorean wrapper in there, but that is not a bad thing. One of the more affordable ones out there is Tatuaje. People who have spent more time with cigars and are looking for something more complex, yet easy smoking, should seek out a Corona Gorda, whose standard size is about 5.5–6 inches with a 50–64 ring gauge depending on the maker. From there, the quality of roll and volume of smoke is the pride of any legitimate cigar maker. Tatuaje is a great brand made in Nicaragua in a factory called "My Father's Cigars." As for the wrapper, find something the color of mahogany or roasted coffee beans.

Tatuaje

WEEKLY POKER GAME: EXPERT

Serious cigar folks are on the hunt for unexpected, distinguished cigars the way you'd look for spicy peppers. They get bolder, hotter, and more dangerous over time, and that's sort of the point. One way to find exotic, unexpected flavors is to seek out cigar shapes that look strange to you. The culebra, which translates to "snake" in Spanish, is a cool, old, traditional cigar. If you were a Cuban roller, you'd get to take home three cigars each day. They wrap them together with string in this weird coil while they are still wet from being made. The result is three twisted cigars that all point in different directions, but they smoke perfectly—one of the most exciting marvels of the cigar world. And it's nice that they can be purchased in threes for sharing with friends. Torpedos are also cool cigars. Sharp-pointed ends allow you to control the ring gauge because it varies depending on where you cut it.

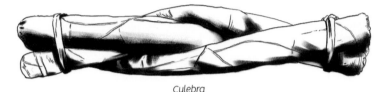

Culebra

When buying cigars for a poker game or going to watch the Masters, go for what's called an A-size. It's the largest cigar demarcation, averaging about 9 inches, and will burn for two to three hours—perfect for a poker game or a quick round of golf. The cigar's exaggerated length allows the cigar maker to create a musical saga within the cigar. You can add a leaf that's there for 20 minutes before turning into something else. When done masterfully, A-size cigars become some of the most complex and high-level smoking experiences. These are usually narrow, about 48–52 ring gauge, since they are coveted by old-school smokers who tend to prefer a tighter gauge. You will see 42–48 as a "go to" for many experts because they have a concentration of wrapper flavor. Illusione out of Nevada uses a factory in Honduras that makes an incredible A-size.

Illusione Epernay Le Voyage

Try This World-Class Cigar: The best cigar producers in most countries are Cuban expats who left the Castro regime, many with little more than a handful of seeds and the clothes on their backs. One such family are the Padróns, who rebuilt their family business in Nicaragua 52 years ago. Today, Padróns are among the premiere makers of top-rated cigars in the world.

WHAT MAKES CUBANS UNIQUE?

Like wine, tobacco is a product of the soil, and dry soil helps produce the right minerality and flavor for cigar tobacco. For this reason, terroir is a huge deal, and Cuba has many different growing regions, which allows it to produce a variety of styles of tobacco. Today, other tobacco countries have caught up. But Cuba was among the first, and that sets its cigars apart. The fact that we aren't allowed to have them unless you bring a few back from Cuba personally is a damn shame.

HOW TO LIGHT UP A STOGIE

Firing up a cigar is one of the most pleasurable moments of your smoking experience, and to enjoy it to its fullest, you need to take your time. To begin, hold your cigar just outside the reach of the flame and rotate it while it roasts. Once it starts to catch, take a puff or two then turn the cigar around and blow. If you are not fully lit, hit it with the flame again. It's going to take 10-25 seconds.

To find a good cigar lighter, look for a butane-powered model. They emit a clean, odorless gas and come in different styles. An inexpensive, disposable Djeep throws enough flame to get the job done, but for something a little slicker, I turned to the crew at *Cigar Aficionado* for some recommendations. Here is what they said:

BLAZER BIG SHOT BUTANE TORCH

Golfers go for a torch lighter, which has a high-pressure, high-temp jet flame that is solid and dependable and fights through a stiff breeze. This Blazer Big Shot will get the job done anywhere, anytime, but while its bulky design is perfect in the outdoors, it doesn't carry well in a suit jacket. **$68**

BRIZARD ETERNAL LIGHTER

For something slick and classy, check out Brizard's line of flamethrowers, which are wrapped in exotic wood casings like rosewood, walnut, and Macassar ebony. It's a good-looking piece that performs. **$130**

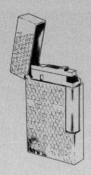

S.T. DUPONT

Go all out with a top-of-the-line FD Dupont Ligne 2,
from Paris. These sexy-as-all-get-out, super-luxe
statement pieces start at around $700 and ascend well
into the five digits with all sorts of unique finishes,
including solid gold. These classics are impeccably
designed and built well enough to pass down through
generations. Oh yeah, they do a damn good job
lighting a cigar, too. **$700**

INDEX

ACKNOWLEDGMENTS

First off, a shout-out to my talented and patient editor, **Mark Weinstein**, for hooking me up with this fantastic project and making me sound smart. I am also grateful to duopress publisher **Mauricio Velázquez de León** for green-lighting the project and providing me with the opportunity to publish my first book.

Huge thanks to **Max McCalman**, a maître fromager, advocate, author, and friend who has taught me most of what I know about cheese. **Eddie Currie** from Puckerbutt, whom I have known since childhood and who has shown me how to enjoy a serious hot sauce, even though them Reaper Squeezins are too ferocious for me. **Ian Burrell** for dealing with my annoying emails and helping me out with the rum chapter. Also thanks and praise to rum gurus **Carlos Seralles** at Don Q, **Gary Nelthropp** from Cruzan, and the notorious **Fred Minnick**, the only person on earth who wears an ascot without irony that I could possibly be friends with. Thanks to El Tesoro brand ambassador **Luis Navarro**, who is lucky enough to rep such a beautiful tequila, and awesome bar manager and tequila geek **Jay Silverman, at Bianco Restaurants** in Phoenix, Arizona. Mezcal Yoda **Lou Banks**, organizer of S.A.C.R.E.D., a not-for-profit that helps small mezcal producers find an audience for their one-of-a-kind expressions. **Clay Whittaker**, whom I drank my way through Tokyo with last year, for his invaluable advice on cigars. **David Savona**, executive editor of *Cigar Aficionado* magazine. Chef **Mike Lippi**, who was garde manger at the opening of New York's Le Bernardin, which received 4 stars from Gael Greene in 1985. Many thanks to my people at **David Burke's King Bar** and the **Rose Room** at the Garden City Hotel, the amazing bartenders who taught me how to do it: **Brian Russell** (even if he didn't give up his red salt margarita recipe), **Leah**, **Lia**, **Kyle**, **Brian Q.**, **Gina**, **Danny**, and all the crazy people that make that beehive buzz. **John D. McCarthy** for the killer tailgating cocktail and for always being a good sport when PR folks get us mixed up. **Clinton Lanier** for his encyclopedia-like beer expertise. Thanks also to **Louis Rozzo**, CEO of F. Rozzo & Sons, who sells fish to over 400 restaurants and whose father hand-delivered seafood to Frank Sinatra, for his oyster guidance. Captain **Tyson Fick**, whose Taku River reds are probably the best salmon on the planet. **Rachael Polhill**, executive chef at Dante in New York City, for schooling me on the difference between a salumi and charcuterie board. And my dear friend, kick-ass guitar player, and charcuterie encyclopedia, **Ron St. George**.

A special mention to my brother, **Brian**, an incredible human being whose selflessness and unwavering family loyalty made it possible for me to finish this book.

And the MVPs of 'em all, my son, **Andrew**, and wife, **Allison**. It can't be easy.

ABOUT THE AUTHOR

John McCarthy is a 25-year publishing veteran who last served as senior managing editor and spirts and cocktail pundit at *Men's Health* magazine. Since his departure in 2016, McCarthy has traveled the world in search of intelligence about fine wine and spirits, amazing adventures, and incredible stories for publications like *Roads & Kingdoms*, *Forbes*, *Men's Health*, *Maxim*, *JW Marriott* magazine, *Bourbon+*, and *Gear Patrol*. When home, McCarthy resides in Queens, New York, and works as spirits guru and mixologist at the Rose Room and David Burke's King Bar at the Garden City Hotel. He is also director of judging of the John Barleycorn Awards.

ABOUT THE ILLUSTRATOR

Stephen Davis is a professional illustrator currently living in Brooklyn, New York. Combining his love and storytelling and dynamic imagery, Stephen naturally pursued a career in illustration. Since graduating from the Savannah College of Art and Design he has worked on numerous illustration projects in the fields of book publishing, music, and advertising. His clients include duopress, Manta Ray Books, Real Reads, and Roc Nation. In his free time, Stephen enjoys martial arts, reading, and taking long walks with his Boston terrier, Bruno.

ALSO AVAILABLE

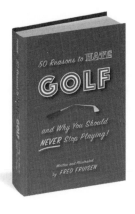

50 REASONS TO HATE GOLF AND WHY YOU SHOULD NEVER STOP PLAYING
By Fred Fruisen

Every golfer has a love/hate relationship with the game. What we love about golf one day, we curse at the next. We've all been frustrated to the point of breaking our clubs or vowing to sell them, announcing our departure from this infuriating sport only to show up at the course the next day, excited to play again. Golf is a game that teases, thrills, torments, and teaches. *50 Reasons to Hate Golf and Why You Should Never Stop Playing* is a hilarious look at this addictive, wonderful, strange, beautiful, exasperating, mystifying sport and the culture surrounding it that people have been obsessed with for more than 500 years.

NEVER COOK BACON NAKED
Compiled by Doreen Chila-Jones

We have all done it: ruined an entire dinner; burned a piece of toast; served raw chicken to our guests. Cooking can be a daunting, frustrating, and hopeless pursuit . . . and

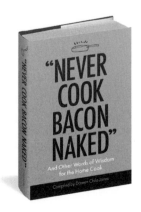

when you are in a pickle, it's time for a little pep talk from some of the biggest cooking and non-cooking experts—people like Julia Child, Thomas Keller, Alice Waters, Truman Capote, Maya Angelou, and many others who, at one time or another, have also scorched their lunch. But remember, as the cookbook author Alana Chernila likes to say, "Homemade food is the opposite of perfection."

SAY WHAT?
By Doreen Chila-Jones

Say What? is a compilation of 670 of the most memorable things that should never have been said. You'll find, of course, quotes from dictators, drug lords, and murderers, but much more shocking are the entries by Nobel Prize winners, religious leaders, and beloved icons. Doreen Chila-Jones has collected hundreds of extraordinary quotes, and everyone is fair game—even Mother Teresa: "I think it is very beautiful for the poor to accept their lot, to share it with the passion of the Christ. I think the world is being much helped by the suffering of the poor people." Say what?